Status of Adivasis/Indigenous Peoples Land Series – 1

GUJARAT

DISCLAIMER

The author and the editorial collective are solely responsible for the contents of this report. The views expressed in this report do not necessarily reflect the views of institutions who supported the research nor Foundation for Ecological Security who supported printing.

Status of Adivasis/Indigenous Peoples Land Series – 1

GUJARAT

Shivani A Patel

A Status of Adivasis/Indigenous Peoples Land Series – 1 : GUJARAT
Shivani A Patel

First Published, 2011

ISBN 978-93-5002-123-1 (Pb)

Published by
AAKAR BOOKS
28 E Pocket IV, Mayur Vihar Phase I, Delhi 110 091
Phone : 011 2279 5505 Telefax : 011 2279 5641
aakarbooks@gmail.com; www.aakarbooks.com

In association with
THE OTHER MEDIA
J 42, IInd Floor, N D S E Part I, New Delhi 110 049
Phones : 011 2462 9372/73 Fax : 011 4104 2271
Email : tom@theothermedia.org

Printed at
Mudrak, 30 A Patparganj, Delhi 110 091

Acknowledgements

The Status Report of Adivasis/Indigenous Peoples (SAIP) has been an important initiative of The Other Media and All India Coordinating Forum of Adivasis/Indigenous peoples. It began with a lot of interest and enthusiasm with a wide consultation among activists, scholars and researchers interested in the Adivasis/Indigenous People's issues. However, the process seemed to have have had its own pace and could not keep up with the expectation of completing the report on time. The present phase of the program has covered, state-wise, issues of land and mining in the Adivasis/Indigenous People's areas.

This report on land issues in Adivasi areas of Gujarat has been prepared by Shivani Patel with the active participation of other friends in that state and members of the Editorial Collective (EC). We gratefully acknowledge the efforts made by Shivani and Michael Mazgaonkar who participated, on behalf of the author, in a workshop organised to review the reports.

Members of the EC went through the reports and gave their valuable comments and suggestions on each of the report. We gratefully acknowledge their contribution that was available at every stage of preparation of the report. The efforts of the EC have been untiringly coordinated by C R Bijoy. The reports owe a lot to his relentless effort to keep in loop everyone concerned towards producing good results out of the reports. At the level of The Other Media, Ravi Hemadri, who worked as the Executive Director of the organisation through most part of the program served as a link between the organisation and the EC. He continued to coordinate the final editing and printing of the reports. We gratefully acknowledge the role played by both C R Bijoy and Ravi Hemadri.

We acknowledge and thank the Adivasi Academy, Tejgarh, Gujarat, and particularly Prof Ganesh Devy, for generously hosting in February, 2008, a two-day workshop of members of the EC and authors to review the draft reports. We thank the members of the Advisory Board of the SAIP, who with their participation in the first consultation and later whenever called upon, gave their inputs to the reports. Thanks are due to Shankar Gopalakrishnan who meticulously put together statistical data and selected literature for SAIP.

Lastly we would like to acknowledge and thank our funders ICCO, Netherlands, and TROCAIRE, Ireland, who supported the program all through the last five years. We are grateful to the Foundation for Ecological Security, Anand, Gujarat, who generously supported the printing of the first phase of reports on land. We thank all of them for being patient with this initiative.

December, 2010

E Deenadayalan
General Secretary

Contents

Index of Tables and Figures

Preface

Eighty-eight million Adivasis and indigenous peoples live in India – approximately one fourth of the world's total indigenous population. Historically self-sufficient, forest based communities with independent cultural identities, they have been subjected to displacement, dispossession and repression for more than a century and are now India's poorest and most marginalised communities. Since the onset of British rule, and in many cases from much earlier, Adivasis and indigenous peoples have been systematically and forcibly dispossessed of the resources of their homelands. In gross violation of democratic practice, social justice and both Constitutional and legal requirements, such dispossession continues to this day. It is also the Adivasis and indigenous peoples who have paid the heaviest price for the current neo-liberal globalisation policies, with their land, resources and forests taken from them for private capital - in the name of 'economic growth.'

These larger processes have been accompanied by the erosion and undermining of cultural identities, leading to a loss of cultural moorings and other markers of ethnicity. Less than half of India's Adivasi communities speak their own language. State and private efforts at 'mainstreaming' and against indigenous faiths, practices and cultural mores have had a devastating impact.

Such trends have not gone unchallenged. Despite growing differentiation, ethnicity has emerged as a strong, consolidating force. Many have organised, often with the help of sympathetic outsiders, to fight against their oppressors and struggle for the control over land and other resources, and for local self government as in parts of Central India. There have been demands for political self-determination and autonomy of varying degrees as in Jharkhand and the Northeast. The state characterises all such struggles as 'Law and Order Problems', and large parts of the central India and the North-east are heavily militarised in the name of 'national security'. In other parts too state repression has been heavy and brutal.

Though these processes are well known to many and particularly to Adivasis and indigenous peoples' movements, there continues to be a dearth of knowledge on the overall status of Adivasis and indigenous peoples in India. The struggle-based mass organisations of Adivasis and indigenous peoples in the Indian sub-continent articulated the need to work towards such a task in the late 1990s. The collective process to fulfill this task was launched in 2005.

The Status of Adivasis/Indigenous Peoples is conceptualised as a series of reports on salient themes affecting the lives of Adivasis/Indigenous Peoples. In the first instance, the series focuses on the situation of land and mining in the tribal tracts of the country. We hope that the series will be effective in not only deliberating upon similar themes of importance to the Adivasi present and future, but also help strengthening linkages amongst movements, activists, scholars and all others who are concerned with the protection of the rights of Adivasis/Indigenous Peoples in the Indian sub-continent.

This series of reports will explore the history, the laws, and the facts, and describe struggles while providing an overview of current realities. The main purpose of these reports is to expand linkages and relationships between movements, scholars, and activists so that the future of the political struggles is informed and forward looking.

In Gujarat
resource
worldwid
contemp
reinforce
marginal
The
the upp
Gujarat
beacon
not part
a power
exclusion
land alie

1.
2.
3.
4.
5.
6.

The hist
largely
interven

Executive Summary

In Gujarat, as in other states, we see the familiar pattern of resource exploitation and wealth extraction that has set a worldwide trajectory for the indigenous experience in the contemporary era. Modern institutions of governance reinforce the power of the dominant classes while further marginalising the original settlers of these lands.

The inequality between the condition of Adivasis and the upper-castes is highly pronounced in Gujarat. Whereas Gujarat boasts of being a highly industrialised state and a beacon of development in contemporary India, Adivasis are not part of this economic 'growth'. Land alienation has been a powerful factor in the economic, social, and political exclusion of Adivasis in Gujarat. Common mechanisms of land alienation include:

1. Private revenue lands alienated by private hands.
2. Private revenue lands alienated by the state.
3. Public revenue wastelands 'developed' by the state and therefore inaccessible to people.
4. Public revenue wastelands co-opted by private parties.
5. Notification of forest on existing individual Adivasi cultivations.
6. Notification of forests on wasteland, placing common property resources including forest produce and grasing land in the hands of the Forest Department.

The historical evidence suggests that these mechanisms exist largely through the selective intervention and non-intervention of the state. State policy is informed by private interests who stand to benefit from this selective intervention. Legislation is implemented when it serves the powerful and ignored otherwise. The non-literate Adivasi, around whom a foreign world of British law had been superimposed, stood little chance at justice against the seasoned lobby of landlords and other vested interests at the time of post-independence land settlement and re-distribution. In the post-Emergency era, the Gujarati elite and state set their eyes on industrialisation, while most Adivasis never had the means for such economic mobility, and instead moved between landed peasant farmer and landless labourer. The state's emphasis on industrialisation thus largely excludes Adivasis.

Today's land scenario in Adivasi areas is a reflection of neglected progressive legislation whose long awaited implementation was forestalled by a new set of reformative measures with a drastically different orientation. The first set of reforms – broadly, those that took place during the time of the erstwhile bilingual Bombay State and the newly formed Gujarat state – were ostensibly designed to protect farmers and agriculture. While Independence marked the beginning of accumulation of wealth and power for Patels, Rajputs, and other upper-castes who became the actual beneficiaries of land reforms, Gujarat's Adivasis steadily lost their rights over their traditional resource base ever since. Requisite surveys were never done in Adivasi areas and thus people's rights over vast tracts of land were never recognised at all. Those lands were then treated as *khalsa*, or wasteland, and reclassified/re-distributed however the state saw fit. This is the case with disputed forest land and private revenue lands which were co-opted by the upper-castes.

The next set of policies reflected Gujarat's vision for industrialisation through a neo-liberal approach which ignored agrarian needs. Gujarat law and policy have been systematically eliminating the safeguards for the land resources of the marginalised. Gujarat pioneered the mechanism for conversion of agricultural land to non-agricultural land – up to 10 hectares can be converted almost instantly (Dholakia 2000). The Gujarat Industries Commissionerate even boasts that the state allows industry to acquire agricultural land for industrial purposes in a 'hassle free' manner (Industry Policy 2003). Laws simplifying conversion of restricted (*navi*) tenure to unrestricted (*juni*) tenure, and conversion of agricultural land to non-agricultural land[1] further facilitate land acquisition from these communities.

Yet Gujarat state often manages to skilfully protect corporate interests. The State government aggressively attempted to illegally renew the lease of the paper company Central Pulp Mills to extract bamboo from the Shoolpaneshwar Wildlife Sanctuary, and simultaneously sanctioned plantation work destroying the fields of Adivasis living in that same forest since prior to declaration of the sanctuary. In 2005 the State government resolved to give away wastelands at throwaway rates for corporate farming, while the government resolution to allot leases for wasteland to the poor and marginalised communities was hardly implemented despite the passage of two decades. While Adivasis make up 76% of people displaced by state infrastructure (mostly dams), the Adivasi share in irrigated cropped area is a mere 5%. Gujarat state's rule of thumb becomes apparent: natural resources may be exploited by the elite class but not wisely used by Adivasis.

Land acquisition for development has myriad impacts on Adivasi lives. Reduction of land holdings and total displacement are among the most visible impacts. The economic consequences are compounded by inferior land quality, an ever emerging phenomenon through the environmental degradation created by mining, industry, large dams and the like. Land and water resources are polluted, salinated, and rendered physically inaccessible due development projects. This has implications for health and agricultural output. These same infrastructure and business endeavours then exploit the cheap labour base created by land alienation itself.

Dispossession of resources and lands at scale has prompted massive social and cultural change within the Adivasi community. The penetration of the cash economy and restricted access to traditional forest and land resources has made seasonal migration a prominent feature in the majority of Adivasi villages. The increased reliance on cash has also forced an increase in unofficial land transfer (via mortgaging, share-cropping, and the like) within the Adivasi community, leading to concentration of wealth amongst a handful of relatively powerful Adivasis to the detriment of the rest.

The shift from strict subsistence agriculture to increased reliance on cash income has had special effects on the status and lives of Adivasi women. Whereas women are limited by cultural norms, men are treated as free agents to move wherever cash might be earned. The role of 'man as the provider' is giving rise to a more rigid gender hierarchy in some Adivasi communities. The integration of Adivasi communities with mainstream Gujarati society is being brought on due to land depletion and the changing economy; this same 'de-tribalisation' has often had a negative influence on Adivasi women with respect to land rights and conditions of life.

1. www.revenuedepartment.gujarat.gov.in as accessed on 24th December 2006.

Author's Note

As Adivasi Mahasabha, a coalition of people's organisations devoted to forest rights among Adivasi communities of Gujarat, we were asked to prepare a 'status' report on land in Adivasi Gujarat. This is a near impossible task because land ownership and use among Adivasis is too dynamic for a static account to be of any meaning. This report instead intends to document in a short space the progression of land distribution and use over time in Adivasi Gujarat, and capture some salient trends in this context. A detailed inventory of the land issue in Gujarat (or any other state) is a monumental task and warrants multiple volumes of documentation. In order to outline the situation within the current space constraints, we rely on a mixed methods approach utilising both quantitative and qualitative data. The limitation of this two-dimensional space, however, is that the rich oral histories of Adivasi communities are not done justice. Archival data presented derive from various institutions antagonistic to the Adivasis, including colonial records and the current Indian government. It is noted that since the contemporary Adivasi land scenario is vastly more externally determined than internally determined, it is ironic, but also necessary, to rely on these external sources for data regarding factors shaping land holdings and the like.

1

The Tribes of Gujarat

Land continues to be the basis of Adivasi communities and economies in Gujarat. The majority of Adivasis in Gujarat are either self-cultivators or work as agricultural labour. No matter where one travels in the eastern Adivasi belt (see Figure 1 for the geographical distribution of scheduled blocks in Gujarat, and Table1 and 2 for the district-wise population, and Scheduled Tribe population within ITDP[2] areas), one will hear stories of land loss during the British period and the Independence era, and land shortage in the contemporary era.

Figure 1. Eastern Adivasi Belt of Gujarat

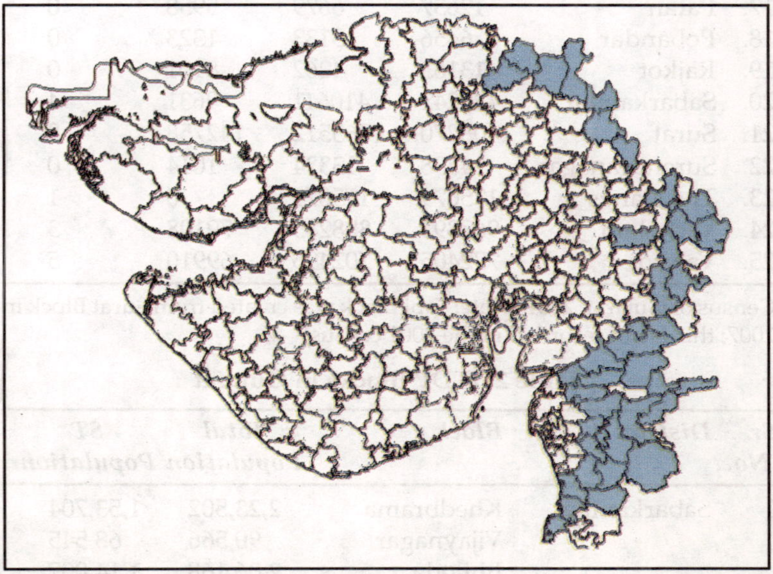

2. Integrated Tribal Development Project

Table 1: District-wise population of Scheduled Tribes (STs)

Sr No.	*District Name*	*Total ST population in District*	*Rural ST popu- lation*	*Urban ST popul lation*	*Number of Scheduled Areas*
1.	Ahmedabad	58035	15334	42701	0
2.	Amreli	3256	1626	1630	0
3.	Anand	22835	12825	10010	0
4.	Banaskantha	205904	196860	9044	0
5.	Bharuch	444043	406442	37601	0
6.	Bhavnagar	7298	2377	4921	2
7.	Dohad	1182509	1136859	45650	1
8.	Gandhinagar	17681	4696	12985	0
9.	Jamnagar	10459	6195	4264	0
10.	Junagadh	18832	13673	5159	0
11.	Kutch	130138	106284	23854	0
12.	Kheda	32394	24831	7563	0
13.	Mehsana	8975	4445	4530	0
14.	Narmada	401654	386465	15189	3
15.	Navsari	591164	534939	56225	0
16.	Panchmahal	556000	541406	14594	4
17.	Patan	12637	6679	5958	0
18.	Pobandar	6456	5133	1323	0
19.	Rajkot	13163	4262	8901	0
20.	Sabarkantha	420242	410611	9631	4
21.	Surat	1408270	1265512	142758	8
22.	Surendranagar	14338	13324	1014	0
23.	The Dangs	175079	175079	0	1
24.	Vadodara	967393	888285	79108	3
25.	Valsad	772405	702495	69910	5

Census of Gujarat, 2001 (Note: Tapi Block was created from Surat Block in 2007; this is not recorded in the 2001 census)

Table 2: ITDP Blocks in Gujarat

Sr. No.	*District*	*Block*	*Total Population*	*ST Population*
1	Sabarkantha	Khedbrama	2,23,502	1,53,704
		Vijaynagar	90,566	68,545
		Bhiloda	2,06,168	1,14,007
		Meghraj	1,41,853	51,612

2	Dahod	Dahod	3,68,184	2,73,469
		Garbada	1,42,448	1,34,378
		Jhalod	3,60,553	3,19,443
		Fathepura	1,85,419	1,70,982
		Limkheda	2,39,357	1,46,764
		Devgadhbariya	2,09,198	4,88,185
		Dharampur	1,31,974	98,288
3	Panchmahal	Santrampura	2,19,041	157,852
		Kadana	1,10,389	80,810
		Ghoghamba	1,89,656	72,123
4	Vadodara	Chhota Udaipur	2,02,697	1,75,480
		Nasvari	1,24,828	1,07,547
		Kawant	1,70,524	1,57,738
		Jetpur Pavi	2,25,894	1,75,183
5	Narmada	Dediapada	1,43,574	1,37,553
		Saghbara	83,633	74,980
		Nandod	2,31,138	1,59,443
		Tilakvada	56,059	29,678
6	Bharuch	Valiya	1,30,587	96,179
		Jhagadiya	1,72,553	1,15,158
7	Tapi	Songadh	2,04,270	1,70,464
		Uchhal	73,012	71,084
		Vyara	2,49,810	2,11,611
		Valod	87,127	64,112
		Nizar	1,05,358	83,843
8	Surat	Mandvi	1,85,911	1,40,800
		Mahuva	1,42,434	1,12,655
		Bardoli	2,10,789	99,213
		Mangrol	1,71,524	90,370
		Umarpada	68,288	65,867
9	Navsari	Vansada	2,01,288	1,81,785
		Chikhli	2,03,014	2,05,275
10	Valsad	Dharampur	1,80,366	1,65,662
		Umargam	2,36,247	1,15,392
		Pardi	4,05,902	1,58,786
		Kaprada	2,02,862	1,89,939

Government of Gujarat, Tribal Development Program, 2008

Adivasis make up 14.9% of the total population in Gujarat, according to the Ministry of Tribal Affairs. Though modern struggles for land rights and the like have attempted to unite Adivasis from all over Gujarat under a single indigenous banner, neither Adivasi culture nor their communities can be considered homogenous. Historically, most Adivasis think of themselves more as members of their subgroup (Bhil, Konkani, Chaudhary, etc; see Table 3 for a listing of the tribes of Gujarat) than they do as 'Adivasi'. This might be due to linguistic and geographical barriers. However, despite this diversity, subsistence economy as well as social customs and proscriptions arising from material culture are a common thread between the various Adivasi groups. These externally observed similarities are perhaps the reason that non-Adivasis have treated all Adivasis as a single entity, which has perpetuated the myth of their homogeneity through time.

Table 3: Tribe wise population of Adivasis in Gujarat

	Tribe	*Total Population 2001*	*% of Adivasi Population*
1.	Barda	775	0.01
2.	Bavacha, Bamcha	4,125	0.06
3.	Bharwad	1,619	0.02
4.	Bhil, Bhil Garasia, Dungri Garasia	3,441,945	46.01
5.	Charan	2,481	0.03
6.	Chaudhri	282,392	3.77
7.	Chodhara	6,786	0.09
8.	Dhanka, Tadvi, Tetaria, Valvi	252,637	3.38
9.	Dhodia	589,108	7.87
10.	Dubla, Talavia, Halpati	596,865	7.98
11.	Gamit, Gamta, Gavit, Mavchi, Padvi	354,362	4.74
12.	Gond, Rajgond	2,152	0.03
13.	Kathodi, Katkari, Dhor: Kathodi, Katk	5,820	0.08
14.	Kokna, Kokani, Kukna	329,496	4.40
15.	Koli	95,655	1.28

16. Koli Dhor, Tokre Koli, Kolcha, Kolgha	48,419	0.65
17. Kunbi	43,292	0.58
18. Naikda, Nayaka: Cholivala, Mota, Nana	393,024	5.25
19. Padhar	22,421	0.30
20. Paradhi	7,189	0.10
21. Pardhi, Advichincher, Phanse Pardhi	2,872	0.04
22. Patelia	109,390	1.46
23. Pomla	819	0.01
24. Rabari	15,417	0.21
25. Rathawa	535,284	7.16
26. Siddi	8,662	0.12
27. Vaghri	16,974	0.23
28. Varli	255,271	3.41
29. Vitola, Kotwalia, Barodia	21,453	0.29
30. Unclassified All Scheduled Tribes	7,481,160	100.00

Census of India, 2001

Most scholars consider the Bhils to be the original inhabitants of Gujarat. Some also argue that the various Adivasi groups in Gujarat were founded through a fissioning of the original Bhil population and admixture with the invading Rajputs. Today, the Bhils are the most populous Adivasi community in Gujarat. They are settled throughout the Eastern Adivasi belt of Gujarat, particularly along the forested banks of the Narmada, Tapi and Mahi rivers. The Bhils are not a homogenous tribe linguistically or culturally, and many subtribes exist throughout Gujarat; intermarriage between Bhils and the invading Rajputs was common. They are mostly land-holding agriculturalists residing in hilly and forested areas. Customarily the various Bhil subtribes prohibit daughters from inheriting land, unless the daughter lives in her native place after marriage or there are no other male heirs. Widows are given usufruct[3] rights to land, which

3. The use of property without legal right.

however is jeopardised if she re-marries (Solanki, 1997). Land is often mortgaged to make purchases; the price is usually fixed on the basis of the quantity of crop sown within the land in question.

The Dublas are settled mostly in Surat, but also can be found in Valsad and Bharuch. They are primarily landless labourers, and display Gujarati acculturation; they are more Hinduised and speak Gujarati. Bhil oral tradition has it that the Dublas (the 'weak') were the Adivasis who opted to stay on in the plains and work in the fields of large non-Adivasi landlords at a time when external pressure drove other Bhil communities to migrate to the forest in search of new territory (Pinto not dated).

The Patelias are considered to be descendants of Rajputs who slowly adopted the Bhil way of life. The Dhodias mostly reside in the plains of Valsad and Surat, and are concentrated in Chikhli and Pardi. They are agriculturalists, but also work as industrial labour. Again, mostly sons inherit land, except in the case of *'Ghar Jamai'*, in which the daughter and her husband live jointly with parents. They have much contact with non-Adivasis, utilise reservations, and have a much higher literacy than other Adivasi populations in the state.

The Chaudharies mostly reside in Surat and Bharuch districts. They tend to be plains-dwelling, and are thought to be highly industrious. Their customary inheritance law does give rights to women over land, where a 'women's own estate' is recognised (Solanki 2000). Dhankas are mostly found in Bharuch, Vadodara, Surat. They rely on agriculture and minor forest produce for sustenance.

The Kuknas (Konkanas, Kuknis, Koknis) are considered to be more traditional peoples, and live in the Dangs, as well as neighboring Surat and Valsad districts. The Warlis also are present in these areas. This community has a concept of 'Vavli', in which some immovable property – usually land – will be set aside specifically for a woman. She is able to dispose of it as she likes. Rathwas reside mostly in the Chhotaudepur area. Naikdas are geographically concentrated in both the south and north of Gujarat – in Panchmahals and Valsad. They tend to be cash-poor, and have a population of about 2.35 lakhs.

The Dangs district consists of a single block that is completely Adivasi (predominantly Bhil) – the only such administrative set-up in the state. The history of indigenous land systems in Gujarat is recorded by academics who have studied the Dangs. These academic accounts resonate with stories told by Bhil elders throughout the Adivasi belt. In the isolated Bhil society of pre-colonial times, the ruling Bhil chiefs and their relatives, the Bhaubands, sat at the top of the hierarchy. Under the Bhil leadership class came ordinary Bhils and a subordinate peasant population composed of the Kuknas, Varlis, and Gamits. The Bhil Chiefs determined who would till which land. Non-Bhils were charged a tax against use of land, which the Bhils did not have to pay. This tax varied based on whether the land was farmed by hand or plough. According to the earliest census data available, the subordinate peasant population actually out-numbered the total Bhil population. Linguistic evidence and oral tradition suggests that the Kuknas migrated from the coastal Konkan region of present day Maharashtra, whereupon they were subjugated by the Bhil Kings despite having more sophisticated cultivation technology and greater food security than the locals. The Kuknas created small fields of ash by burning forest debris, on which they would then sow seeds of *nagli* (a millet type grain) or rice. Once the rains began, they would plough adjacent plots and transplant the seedlings from the ash plot to the tilled soil. Kuknas employed this method in the valleys, as their farming technology was more suited for level ground. The Bhils and Varlis relied on swidden agriculture that required no ploughing. They would often select plateau sites. Seeds of similar millets were sown in the ash, and then simply left to the magic of the monsoon, which would yield a harvest by the end of the season. Each year a new site would be selected. Because of the less fertile soil of these higher sites, and the less productive cultivation method they used, Bhils and Varlis tended to have proportionately smaller yields than the Kuknas. As a result, the Bhils and the Varlis foraged and hunted to supplement their food supplies.

The Adivasi relationship with land has never been based on the concept of land as a simple two-dimensional productive area that can be marked for ownership. Forest foraging for foodstuffs such as *mahuva* flowers, honey; fish and small game; as well as household construction materials such as teak wood and bamboo were integral aspects of land use that were not subject to proprietary rights or inherited by any authority. Various cultural practices such as ritual food exchange also exist, organised around the cyclical seasons of nature.

2

The Processes of Land Alienation

State-fostered processes, in particular the process of settlement of rights, have been the primary cause of Adivasi land alienation. The very nature of state-declared, immutable boundaries for land ownership violated traditional Adivasi land systems. Subsequent land reforms, which were rendered necessary by the seizure of Adivasi ancestral lands in the first place, ironically became a springboard for further alienation of Adivasi land. These processes are discussed in this section.

2.1 Survey and Settlement

Permanent agricultural settlements hardly existed among the Adivasis of Gujarat before the British era. The Bhils, the most numerous and widespread Adivasi community in Gujarat, relied on a mixed economy of shifting cultivation complemented by hunting and forest foraging (see the earlier section for information relating to various Adivasi communities of Gujarat). In the pre-Independence era, the Adivasis were by no means confined to the mountainous terrain in the eastern part of Gujarat State; they were spread through the plains and their territory spanned some of the most fertile land in the region (See Jani and Ganguly 2000; Pinto not dated). In the pre-British era, *talukdari* tenure, in which the occupant would have non-inheritable rights to minerals, mines and trees, was common (Modak 1932). The Adivasis were not fully isolated from non-Adivasis, but were also not fully culturally, economically, and politically integrated into the Gujarati mainstream. While the rulers of the princely estates decided the area open for cultivation and for grasing, and collected taxes from the Adivasis, they were reportedly more liberal than the British. Even today, elder generations remember that the princes allowed the Adivasis to do what they pleased within their designated territory. Cultivation, along with other aspects of life, was regulated more by the chieftains – especially amongst the Bhils. The Bhil Chieftains and the ruling Princes exercised parallel authority.

Eventually the British did wrest control of some of the territories occupied by Adivasis (see Figure 2 for pre-Independence rulers and Table 4 to understand the modern divisions of pre-Independence territories). The British, primarily concerned with maximising revenue, had a vested interest in the systematic settlement of title over lands under their control. They promoted the *ryotwari* system – in which

Figure 2. Pre-Independence Boundaries of Gujarat

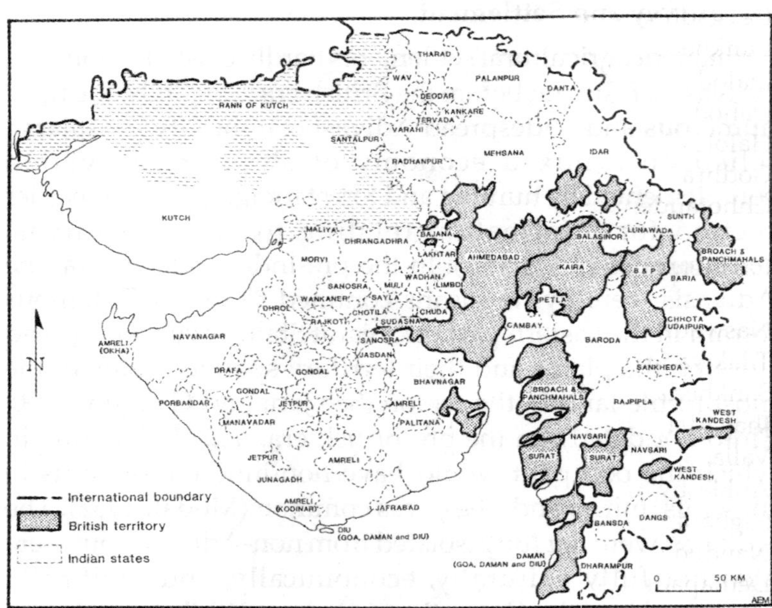

(Wood 1984)

the cultivator directly held land and paid taxes to the state – seeing its successful execution in Madras. The British found landlords to be inefficient in collecting land revenue, and therefore preferred occupancy and settlement to be directly with the cultivator (Modak 1932). While the British prioritised settling farmers, many princely control areas remained unsettled until Independence.

Table 4: Pre-Independence and Post-Independence Block Distribution

Present Block	*Present District*	*Controlling Authority Pre-Independence*
Palanpur	Banaskantha	Palanpur Princely Estate
Danta	Banaskantha	Danta Princely Estate
Bhiloda	Sabarkantha	Idar Princely Estate
Meghraj	Sabarkantha	Idar Princely Estate
Khedbrahma	Sabarkantha	Idar Princely Estate
Vijaynagar	Sabarkantha	Vijaynagar Princely Estate
Santrampur	Panchmahal	Sant Princely Estate
Devgadhbaria	Dahod	Baria Princely Estate
Limkheda	Dahod	Baria Princely Estate
Jhalod	Dahod	Sanjeli/British
Dahod	Dahod	British
Halol	Dahod	British
Godhra	Panchmahal	British
Chhotaudepur	Vadodara	Chhotaudepur Princely Estate
Pavi Jetpur	Vadodara	Chhotaudepur Princely Estate
Naswadi	Vadodara	Naswadi/Ghadboriad
Tilakwada	Narmada	Vadodara Princely Estate
Sankheda	Vadodara	Vadodara Princely Estate
Jhagadia	Bharuch	Rajpipla Princely Estate
Valia	Bharuch	Rajpipla Princely Estate
Ankleshwar	Bharuch	Rajpipla Princely Estate
Sagbara	Narmada	Rajpipla Princely Estate
Nandod	Narmada	Rajpipla Princely Estate
Dediapada	Narmada	Rajpipla Princely Estate
Vyara	Surat	Vadodara Princely Estate

Valod	Surat	Vadodara Princely Estate
Sogadh	Surat	Vadodara Princely Estate
Uchchhal	Surat	West Khandesh (British)
Nizar	Surat	West Khandesh (British)
Mahuva	Surat	Vadodara Princely Estate
Mandvi	Surat	Vadodara Princely Estate
Songadh	Surat	Vadodara Princely Estate
Mangrol	Surat	Vadodara Princely Estate
Bardoli	Surat	British
Chikhli	Navsari	British
Pardi	Valsad	British
Umbergaon	Valsad	British
Dharampur	Valsad	Dharampur Princely Estate
Vansda	Navsari	Vansda Princely Estate
Dangs	Dangs	British

Banaskantha District

The Bhils and Garasias reside in Banaskantha district of Gujarat. The region is rocky and forested, and includes areas formerly part of two Princely States, Palanpur and Danta, in pre-Independence India. In Palanpur, two types of landholders existed: common cultivators within the *ryotwari* system, and an elevated class of cultivator who held various reward lands. The former Palanpur State had three different methods of assessing taxes: the size of land tilled, crop share, and the plough tax system, of which the last was the most common. In the plough tax system, a cultivator was made to pay a fixed lump sum per plough and the number of bullocks owned. The villages in the former Danta Princely State were not surveyed or settled prior to Independence. The crop share taxation system prevailed in this area, and the state also taxed minor forest produce. Though the prince had the power to arbitrarily raise prices and evict tenants without cause, neither happened frequently (Trivedi 1993).

Adivasi land holdings were surveyed and settled after Independence in 1956-57. All existing cultivations were regularised at that time. Many Adivasi cultivators are the lawful owners of some land, in practice, but the Land Ceiling

Act and tenancy reform did not have much impact on their conditions (Trivedi 1993).

Sabarkantha District

The densely forested and hilly block of Vijaynagar in Sabarkantha district was formerly a princely state. In the remote villages of this area, the village headman collected a share of the crop as tax. The areas of Bhiloda, Khedbrahma, and Meghraj made up the former Princely state of Idar. It was the largest state in what is today Sabarkantha district. Though this region was inhabited by Bhils, non-Adivasis were encouraged to settle on uncultivated wastelands in the north of the region. A share of harvested crops was collected as tax. Like Vijaynagar, scattered settlements and isolated houses forced the state to rely on village headmen (called Mukhi Gameti) to collect the tax. In return, these local agents of the state were given land free of tax and cash payment. The amount collected was determined by various methods, including (in order of prevalence) the extent of land cultivated, the number of ploughs, and the quantity of the crop. In the large but distant areas at the periphery of the state, a fixed amount was paid to the state via middlemen. Two-thirds of the area of Idar was controlled by *Jagirdars*, who were grantees of Princely land. These *Jagirdars* were known to be extravagant, paid next to nothing in tax, and opposed any moves towards land reform. They eventually destroyed much of the forest in the region. The Idar state was first surveyed and settled in 1868 and was resurveyed in the early 20th century. The occupants of these lands were allowed to sell, lease, or mortgage their land if they so chose, regardless of which category of land or tax was relevant to them (Trivedi 1993).

The transition from the princely states to the Indian State posed some classical problems. In Jamgadh village in Sabarkantha, a 500 hectare plot of land was privately owned by a *jagirdar*. Threatened by the approaching abolition of his rights to that land, the *jagirdar* had the forest on it cleared and sold it to the local Adivasis, but did not get the land transfer registered in the land records. This land was then marked as revenue wasteland, which later came under the control of the Forest Department. The Adivasis, despite possessing receipts as proof of their purchase, became encroachers in the eyes of the law. This is a familiar pattern throughout the state (Iyengar 2002).

Panchmahal and Dahod Districts

The area of Santrampur was part of the Sant Princely State. The *ryotwari* system dominated in this area. Settlement and occupancy rights had been recognised by the Sant state, but sales to individuals other than direct heirs were subject to official approval. Devgadhbaria and Limkheda were part of the former Baria Princely State. The *ryotwari* system was in place, with taxation rates determined on the basis of land fertility. The state charged a fee for recognising occupancy rights. The Baria Princely State had certain measures in place to mitigate the causes and impacts of land alienation. When an individual was forced to sell his land due to debt or other circumstances of duress, a small plot would be preserved in his name so as to allow him to maintain his status as a farmer. Furthermore, sales and mortgages of land by the owner had to be approved by a revenue authority. Jhalod fell partially into the Sanjeli Princely State; again, the *ryotwari* system prevailed and occupancy rights were conveyed directly by the state. The remainder of Jhalod, along with Dahod, Halol and Godhra, came under British control in 1853, when Maratha rulers handed over the territory. Survey and settlement of these lands therefore took place according to the Bombay Land Revenue Code of 1879. The land records were revised between 1906-07 and 1926-27. A complex system of revenue collection was instituted here, in which a collection hierarchy was created on a contract basis. In some cases, village headmen assessed how much villages could pay, and were allowed to operate on five-year contracts on the condition that there was an annual increase in rent income.

This income was then turned over to 'Revenue Farmers', who stood at the top of the district hierarchy. Social caste-based taxation was also employed in some areas. In yet other areas, a crop share tax system was in place, in which one-third to one-half of all produce was declared to be the property of the state (Trivedi 1993).

Dahod was a special case. This area was primarily settled by Bhils who could not afford high tax impositions. When the state attempted to settle the region, about 11,000 acres of cultivated land was abandoned by the people, which subsequently led to a decrease in the human as well as cattle population. Similarly in Jhalod, 5,000 acres of land was abandoned by indigenous cultivators at the time of settlement. The state regretted the loss of taxable income due to the 28.5% population decrease and increase in fallow land. The famine of 1899-1900 also contributed to economic loss in the area, and the condition of peoples today show that these historical incidents have had a lasting impact on this region.

Vadodara District

Lands in Chhotaudepur were surveyed while still a princely state, but the settlement system was based on the British mechanism. The survey and settlement took place between 1909 and 1919, and the occupants were given rights similar to those conferred by the Bombay Land Revenue Code (BLRC) of 1879. But these rights were not recognised in the official record because the 1913 amendment to the BLRC was not extended to the state. The *Darbar*, or local state, had oversight in land transfers; this was purportedly to protect weaker land holders from land alienation due to debt. The British territory included the Ghadboriad and Naswadi Estates in the Rewakantha Agency. Farmers were taxed on the basis of various assessment methods – according to the number of ploughs, area of land-holding, quality and productivity of land, and by crop size (Trivedi 1993).

Bharuch and Narmada District

Though a part of the Rajpipla Princely state, settlement procedures in these districts were based on the British system. The *ryotwari* system was first introduced in 1885, and by 1890 the settlement was complete in a majority of villages. Revisions were made in 1910. Sagbara Estate was given out for cultivation by the Rajpipla Princely State, but was not surveyed at that time (Trivedi 1993). The Gujarat government was the first to survey these lands. By the time the state began settling the lands, other objectives coloured the process. Vast tracts of land were taken over by the forest department, under the pretext that they were unsettled wasteland (see details on the ARCH case below for further information). Large areas of Nandod and Dediapada blocks were used as game preserves and the *Maharaja* set aside parts of these as shooting reserves. More details on the settlement in this district follow this section.

Surat District

The former British areas were all surveyed and settled according to the BLRC. In the area falling under the former Vadodara state, land was given to the highest bidder who would in turn extract tax from tenant farmers. Under this system, cultivators had neither fixed assessment nor secure tenure. Tax according to the *Bigha* was introduced after the survey. Reportedly, cultivators would migrate to British-administered areas to escape arbitrary tax-assessment as a result. Where Bhils and Nayakas were stronger, practically no tax could be collected. Officials saw that their ability to extract tax was limited by the capabilities of people to pay, and settled the land between 1880 and 1901 accordingly. Mostly a *ryotwari* system was put in place in Baroda, but the *Narwadi-Bhagdari* and *Ankabandhi* systems were also present. The former involved fixing a tax for the entire village, which a *Narwadar* would collect; farmers were tenants of the *Narwadar* and not the state. The *Bhagdari* system required cultivators to pay jointly, based on customary responsibility.

In the *Ankabandhi* system, traditional leaders were left to manage tax collection every few years from the entire village. In 1938, a Backward Classes Land Protection Act was enacted to protect Adivasis and others by restricting transfers from Adivasis to non-Adivasis, though transfer among Adivasis was allowed (Trivedi 1993).

Valsad District

Chikhli, Pardi, Dharampur and Umergaon were administered by the British and surveyed and settled according to the provisions of the BLRC. Both Dharampur and Vansda were Princely States, and were inhabited mostly by Adivasis. In Dharampur, the *ryotwari* system prevailed, and the state collected tax according to the quality and quantity of the land holding. This area also included a rich, dense jungle. The last revision survey here was completed in 1919, but only in a few villages. Vansda has a similar history, though the last revision settlement was done in 1923. Vansda also enacted the Agriculturalists' Relief Act and the Alienation of the *Raniparaj* (forest people) Cultivators Land Act. The Revenue Officer was required to approve all land transactions, and measures were also taken to prevent usurious interest being levied on loans to the Adivasis.

Parsis, Brahmins, and Banias were the major non-Adivasi land owners in this district. On average, the Adivasis here have land holdings between 20 *gunthas* and 3-4 acres in area. Many could not pay the purchase price of the land, and are therefore landless.

Dangs District

This heavily forested and hilly district is dominated by Adivasis, and consists of a single block. The area was ruled by Bhil Chiefs and Naiks. The Dangis are known to have practiced shifting-cultivation, for which the plough tax was the most appropriate method of revenue extraction. The Kuknas and Warlis were subject to taxation, whereas the ruling Bhil kings, Naiks, and their kin collected the revenue.

The British exploited the forest areas by virtue of leases granted to them by the Bhil Kings. Though the Bhil kings were the original settlers and remained, in their view, in control of the forests and of revenue collection, the British simultaneously swindled the Bhils and *de facto* placed the forest lands under British control by creating paper records. Thus, the lease of 1842 only gave the British the right to extract timber in exchange for paying a fee to the Bhil kings. But, by 1862, the lease placed additional conditions on the Bhil Chiefs, including a bar on entry without the permission of the Forest Officer, restrictions on the lands left for cultivation, and restrictions on sale of land without sanction of the British government. By 1879, the forests of the Dangs were classified into protected and reserved categories, and cultivation was only permitted in the former. Slowly the rights of the Dangis to the forest were expropriated, even as Bhil power in the area diminished. On the grounds that the Bhil kings were oppressing the cultivators, British agents inserted themselves as middlemen collecting tax, breaking the chain between the people and the Bhil rulers (Hardiman 2003). No private ownership of land existed; Dangis simply cultivated the protected areas up until 1970 when the government of Gujarat conferred occupancy rights and areas to farmers based on family size. (Trivedi 1993). While the livelihood basis of Dangis rests on land, it does not rest solely on agriculture. Utilisation of forest resources also contributes to income and livelihood.

2.2 Post-Independence Tenancy Framework

The Indian nation-state inherited and accepted the British land tenure system. While the British were interested in land distribution and settlement amongst Adivasis so as to convert the masses into tax-paying subjects, the nascent Indian state emphasised poverty reduction and self-reliance as national goals. The first Five Year Plan of 1951 ostensibly promoted land reforms with an emphasis on distributive justice and increased productivity (Koshy 1974).

Gujarat was part of the merged bilingual Bombay State until 1st May 1960. Most of Gujarat's legislation relating to land reform was crafted while Gujarat was still part of the Bombay state; only minor adjustments took place after the creation of a separate Gujarat. Harshad Trivedi suggests that there were two major objectives of land reforms in the post-independence era. The first was to remove 'impediments between the land and its tiller, as they are harmful to agricultural production'. The second was to 'remove all forms and elements of exploitation and social injustice built-in within the pre-independent agrarian relationships'. (Trivedi 1993). In effect, 1) restricting tenure, 2) tenancy reform, 3) land ceilings, and 4) abolishing intermediaries were the legal avenues through which agrarian reform was instituted.

When Adivasis laid claim to land during the era of tenancy reform, the Deputy Collector had the authority to take a decision on the disputed land. Landlords were then free to appeal to the Collector if a decision had been taken against them. The landlord could further go to the Special Secretary in-charge of land disputes if he received an unfavourable decision from the Collector. Finally, the landlord could appeal to the civil courts. Landlords also had other tricks up their sleeves. By government order, tenants could not take possession of lands with standing crops in the field. As a result, the non-Adivasi land owner would continuously till the field in such a manner that there would be no window in which the land would be left fallow, effectively barring the legal transfer of possession to the Adivasi. Landlords (who were largely non-Adivasis) were more affluent and educated and thus had vast scope to appeal decisions. In contrast, Adivasis were particularly helpless in legal matters due to historical isolation and illiteracy.

Bombay Land Revenue Code and Restricted Tenure (73 A)

The majority of the Adivasi areas in Gujarat fell under the rule of Princely States prior to independence. Since the independent Bombay State chose to maintain the Bombay

Land Revenue Code (BLRC) drafted under the Bombay Presidency, the Princely territories had to be integrated with the rest of the State according to the settlement rules and procedure set by the BLRC. It seems that the state was especially concerned with the 'scientific' settlement of lands.

As the revenue the British collected from farmers was contingent on the ability of a cultivator to give, the British had a vested interest in seeing high productivity in agricultural areas, and hence settled farmers from Kheda District in the Adivasi areas of Panchmahal (Jani and Ganguly 2000). The migration of non-Adivasi money lenders and businessmen into these areas had a devastating effect on the Adivasi population, forcing many people to abandon their lands to avoid tax and the like. The original BLRC provided for unrestricted transfer of land, but the impact on Adivasis forced the British to amend the Code to prevent the alienation of Adivasi land (Jani and Ganguly 2000). The 1901 amendment incorporated section 73 A in the Code. Section 73 A was viewed as a protective measure for economically marginalised people who were prone to land alienation due to impoverishment. This amendment empowered the state government to notify areas where transfer of occupancies would require the prior consent of the district collector, though only areas where original survey settlement had not yet taken place could be so notified. Section 79A built in an enforcement mechanism: the power to summarily evict any person unlawfully occupying/possessing such lands (See Modak, 1932 for details on section 73A). Popularly, land falling under this type of restricted tenure is called '*navi sharat*' (new condition), versus the '*juni sharat*' (old condition), unrestricted tenure lands.

At the time of the amendment, about 50% of the total revenue to be collected was overdue. The colonial government primarily wanted to avoid the creation of an unduly large class of landless people who would then rely on the state for meeting their needs. Thus the state also inserted a provision into Section 68 that allowed the Collector to sanction occupations of land under certain conditions. This new, restricted tenure conditionality protected Adivasis residing in areas that had not yet been settled, and also Adivasis who were granted government wasteland under Section 68. Unfortunately, these provisions were not widely applied nor widely well known (for example, see discussion on the *Pardi Satyagraha*). In 1961 the Gujarat government issued a separate notification declaring Section 73A applicable in all Scheduled Areas of Gujarat, excluding non-STs residing in the area. The prior surveys of most blocks in these areas were deemed to be invalid since they were not done according to the Bombay Land Revenue Code. As Dahod, Umergaon, and Jhalod were part of formerly British controlled areas, it has been impossible to enforce 73A in these areas. Whereas the Maharashtra Restoration of Lands to Scheduled Tribes Act in 1974 specifically granted powers to retroactively address the problem of lands alienated after 1957, the Gujarat law did not do the same. Therefore, lands alienated before the 1961 notification of Section 73 remain alienated in Gujarat state in both surveyed and unsurveyed areas.

The Bombay Land Revenue (Gujarat Second Amendment) Act, 1980 introduced further restrictions on the land transfers by Adivasis. All Adivasi lands were declared inalienable, regardless of whether the transfer was to another Adivasi or to a non-Adivasi. The Revenue Department of Gujarat began maintaining records of cases registered under Section 73A in 1980 (Jani and Ganguly 2000). Currently, section 73A of the Bombay Land Revenue Code as applicable to Gujarat contains the following provisions:

73A: Restricts the occupant's right of transfer by making transfers liable to state sanction. In practice, land transfers between Adivasis and non-Adivasis were particularly marked as suspect.

73AA: Prohibits land transfer from Adivasis to Adivasis from the date of notification into force of the amendment. Land alienation from an Adivasi to another Adivasi that took place between 1960 and 1980 was to be upheld. This is in contrast to other states, where such transfers were retroactively cancelled.

73AB: Allows Adivasi occupants to mortgage their lands to the state government or certain institutions in order to receive loans. Such Adivasi lands can be legally auctioned by credit cooperative societies and banks to recover loans.

73AC: Places decisions made by the Collector regarding Section 73A and AA outside the jurisdiction of the civil courts.

73AD: Bars registration of documents in any cases of land transfer by Adivasi occupants without the sanction of the collector.

In practice, the impact of 73A is difficult to measure on the ground. It is impossible to know how many non-Adivasis might have made efforts to co-opt Adivasi land had the provision not been in place. Therefore to assess the efficacy of 73A, we can only look at the theoretical soundness of the law and the outcome of cases in which the law was actually invoked. Many feel that the provision does not offer much *de facto* protection against land alienation. Provision 73AB has been widely criticised as undermining the intention of the entire 73A section of the BLRC; whether land is mortgaged to and ultimately alienated to private parties or the state, the farming family will face the same fate of landlessness or land shortage. It is important to note that land records at the district level Revenue Departments are not reliable and re-drawing of district boundaries and shortage of staff have compounded the problem. When various collectors were asked about the incidence of land disputes involving Section 73A, most responded that it was hardly invoked. The Sabarkantha District Collector claims that no cases have ever been filed in the district under 73-A; the Valsad Collector claims that they have records only for 1997 to the present, and in this period a total of 36 cases have been filed under 73-A (in which two-third of the cases were decided against Adivasi claimants). The SDO of Ankleshwar block has records showing that transfer of roughly 1,730 hectares of land to Adivasi claimants was pending in 1981. As of today, transfer of 1,725 hectares of land is still pending in the block. The Bharuch District Collector reports that of 41 land cases (involving nearly 66 hectares of land) filed under section 73-A after 2001, only one case was decided in the favour of the Adivasi owner. These low numbers reflect the fact that various back-door methods are being used to transfer Adivasi land. In 1996 the state government passed a Government Resolution that allows for the conversion of new tenure lands to old tenure lands, thereby creating a loophole through which Adivasi lands may be alienated.

According to the official state record, 47,926 cases of land disputes regarding 1,40,324 acres have been filed by Adivasis in Gujarat state. Of those, 40,281 cases were decided in favour of Adivasis, and in 21,834 cases land was restored to the Adivasi party. A total of 67,862 acres of land were thus restored to Adivasis through legal action according to the Directorate of Land Reforms (Ministry of Rural Development 2006).

Jani and Ganguly (2000) made a study of the protected tenure of Adivasis under 73A of the BLRC. They observed three mechanisms through which Adivasi land was alienated: power-of-attorney, conversion of agricultural land into non-agricultural land, and abuses of the Bombay Tenancy Act. The use of power-of-attorney involves an Adivasi giving legal powers over his land to another party – an Adivasi or non-Adivasi – for a given period of time. However, these powers are usually never transferred back, and it becomes difficult to prove in court that the land originally belonged to another. Household economy and the current development paradigm play a strong role in land alienation. Legal recourse is hardly a solution since Adivasis do not have the financial means, or the awareness, to take such action. 86.4% of the houses surveyed in their sample were land holders at some time. Of those 3,187 landed households, 224 cases of land alienation were observed. Land was sold outright in 92 cases, mortgaged in 130 cases and submerged in 2 cases. Land alienation due to acquisition was a key concern.

Moneylenders in Vadodara district have posed classic problems. The 73A provisions were evaded by them in various ways. There were cases where they would thwart the implementation of Section 73A by saying that they had lent money to non-Adivasis, because the exact surname of the debtor does not appear in the 5th Schedule (Trivedi 1993). Even when lands were in the ownership of Adivasis, they are often mortgaged so that the land is effectively out of their control; in Naswadi block, 75% of the land is reported to have been lost in this way. Jani and Ganguly found that 9.3% of households had experienced land alienation among three sample villages (2000).

In 1969 thousands of applications were made in Vadodara to restore land in the name of Adivasis under section 73A. However, the non-Adivasi land owners got stay orders from the civil court, barring the restoration of an estimated 12 lakh acres to Adivasi farmers (Trivedi 1993). After the amendments in 1980 to the land revenue code, the interference of civil courts was banned.

Finally, while 73A has had little impact on protecting Adivasis from land alienation, it has had a major impact on the compensation extended to Adivasis during land acquisition for various 'public works'. Because Adivasi lands are not officially transferable, corporations use the government as a middle-man to acquire these lands at throw-away rates. Simultaneously, non-Adivasis living in the same area are free to bargain with these corporations and thus get much higher compensation for the same quality and quantity of land. This further aggravates the economic disparity between Adivasis and non-Adivasis, and makes it more difficult for Adivasis to compete in the market to purchase new land and the like.

The Many Incarnations of the Bombay Agricultural Tenancy Act

Agitations by the Kisan Sabha in Gujarat played an important role in securing the first legislation to regularise the rights of tenants in the merged Bombay state, the Bombay Tenancy Act of 1939 (Yagnik 1950). Though Indulal Yagnik and others made significant efforts on the ground to spread awareness about the act, implementation met with little success. Under the Tenancy Act, tenants who had occupied the land for six years or more were considered 'protected tenants'. This gave tenants secured tenure, ceiling on rental price, rights over homes and trees, and protection from arbitrary evictions. M.B Desai surveyed the impact of the earlier Bombay Tenancy Act and found a decline of land ownership in the northern part of the state and an increase of land ownership in South Gujarat, suggesting that economic conditions had a stronger influence on land ownership outcomes than tenancy legislation itself. He also found that the progressive land reforms of that era were insufficient to uplift the lower classes, including the Adivasis (Desai 1956). In 1956, the concept of '*khede teni jamin*', or Land to the Tiller, was institutionalised by the Bombay state. The Tenancy Act was amended to deem all self-cultivating tenants – ordinary, permanent, or protected – owners of their respective land from 1st April 1957, which is thus known as Tillers Day. Ceiling restrictions according to the area applied. The Agricultural Lands Tribunal determined the purchase price, and the *mamlatdar* was given power to resolve disputes regarding occupancy. In backward areas, the maximum price was fixed at 80 times the revenue assessment of the land (compared to a maximum of 200 times fixed as the assessment in areas not falling under this notification).

It was common for eligible tenants to 'lose' the opportunity of becoming official owners of the land – particularly in Adivasi areas. Passive land loss sometimes occurred by failing to comply with the procedure to get land. This happened in the form of non-attendance to official court proceedings regarding transfer of rights or non-payment of the cash instalments. See Tables 5 and 6 for survey data regarding how many tenants actually got land and how many people lost land because they could not pay the assessment

Table 5: Adivasi Land Lost Due to Tenancy Reform

District	*Name of Adivasi Taluka*	*The no. of Adivasis who were unable to pay the purchase price*	*% of total surveyed*	*The amount they would have had to pay*	*Average amount that Adivasi was unable to pay*	*No. of Adivasis who voluntarily surrendered their lands*	*% of total surveyed*	*The area they voluntarily alienated*	*No. of Adivasis who lost land on the grounds that their landlord personally cultivated*	*Area alienated*
Panchmahal	Jhalod	303	5.66	64183.00	211.83	3	0.06	1	23	44
	Dahod	593	4.39	159769.00	269.42	4	0.03	4	13	16
	Santrampur	0	0.00	0.00	-	0	0.00	0	0	0
	Limkheda	11	0.67	3280.00	298.18	0	0.00	0	0	0
	Devgadhbaria	240	6.19	38986.00	162.44	0	0.00	0	0	0
Vadodara	Chhotaudepur	596	5.42	151037.00	253.42	1315	11.22	1137	177	358
	Tilakwada	271	7.64	61827.00	228.14	0	0.00	0	52	103
Bharuch	Jhagadia	1200	11.84	1455240.00	1212.70	502	5.32	1234	39	80
Surat	Vyara	1578	4.66	113266.00	71.78	118	0.36	49	0	0
	Mahuva	1298	9.12	184805.00	142.38	15	0.12	18	118	86
	Songadh	670	3.14	75000.00	111.94	0	0.00	0	89	418
	Valod	468	5.19	195107.00	416.90	89	1.03	68	142	121
	Bardoli	199	19.34	82323.00	413.68	39	4.49	61	22	13
Valsad	Pardi	1215	6.22	53797.00	44.28	1227	6.28	628	775	856
	Total/Average	8642	6.39	2638620.00	295.16	3312	0.02	3200	1450	2095

Trivedi 1993

Table 6: Adivasi Revenue Land Regularised under the Bombay Tenancy Act

District	*Name of divasi Taluka*	*No. of Adivasis were given occupancy rights as deemed purchasers*	*The Area brought under their control (ha)*	*Average area per Adivasi farmer over surveyed talukas*	*Average area per Adivasi farmer over surveyed portions of the district*
Panchmahal	Jhalod	5046	2042	0.40	0.73
	Dahod	12917	13251	1.03	
	Santrampur	274	193	0.70	
	Limkheda	1641	998	0.61	
	Devgadhbaria	3640	3280	0.90	
Vadodara	Chhotaudepur	10406	9109	0.88	0.94
	Tilakwada	3278	3278	1.00	
Bharuch	Jhagadia	8933	20429	2.29	2.29
Surat	Vyara	32285	69292	2.15	1.09
	Mahuva	12935	9241	0.71	
	Songadh	20675	11584	0.56	
	Valod	8555	10934	1.28	
	Bardoli	830	626	0.75	
Valsad	Pardi	18315	7825	0.43	0.43
Total/Average		139730	162082	1	1

Trivedi 1993

price or faced other problems related to tenancy settlement. As a gesture to ameliorate the situation, the Government of Gujarat attempted to give potential applicants a second chance by extending the deadline and also framed rules for the Agriculturalist Loans Act to assist in making late payments on the land in question. The Act was more aggressively amended again in 1973 in order to improve possibility for implementation. This time, lands surrendered by tenants became the property of the state rather than coming under the possession of the landlord. The timeframe within which claims to land were to be made was further extended. A strict ban was imposed on non-agriculturalists' ability to purchase agricultural land – so anyone earning over Rs. 5,000 from some other activity was unable to purchase land. Purchasers were required to live within 8 km of the agricultural land in question. Landlords of Adivasi tenants (and of other scheduled communities) could not terminate the tenancy due to personal cultivation or diverting the land for non-agricultural use. Agricultural land tribunals were also empowered to issue temporary injunctions to prevent landlords from evicting tenants.

However, Adivasis faced a very different picture of the social 'law' set down by the powerful land-owning elites, against which the rule of law stood little chance. Land to the Tiller promoted active land alienation by the elites. Indulal Yagnik of the *Kisan Sabha*, in his autobiography, states, 'The government was making a claim on the one hand to accept the slogan *Land to the tiller* and to implement it, yet on account of its law regarding tenancy, thousands of true tenants were being driven away from the land or they were compelled to part with a 50% crop share as if they were agricultural labourers' (Yagnik 1950). In all corners of Gujarat one hears stories of how land was alienated on a mass scale due to the institution of the Tenancy Act. Upon the 1954 enactment, some 500,000 farmers throughout Gujarat received notices to surrender their lands to their landlords (Desai 2002).

In addition, Pinto's study of the land records of Bhamadia village show that by 1957, just prior to the time when the Land to the Tiller movement was legally begun, mass transfer of land from Adivasi to non-Adivasi names took place (Pinto, not dated). Amongst the original Bhil settlers of Kodh village, only 32% now own land, and a majority of those land owners possess less than 6 acres (Judge 1999). In effect, Land to the Tiller provided a legal avenue to regularise land in the name of anyone who could provide some proof that he or she was a tenant of some land. Parsis, Patels, and other powerful groups used this law as a mechanism to regularise co-opted land in their names rather than in that of the original Adivasi cultivator. Thus, because of tenancy reform, Adivasis who were *de facto* tenants legally became mere agricultural labourers while *de facto* landlords became legal owners of land.

Figure 3: Land regularisation due to the Tenancy Act among Adivasis and Non-Adivasis

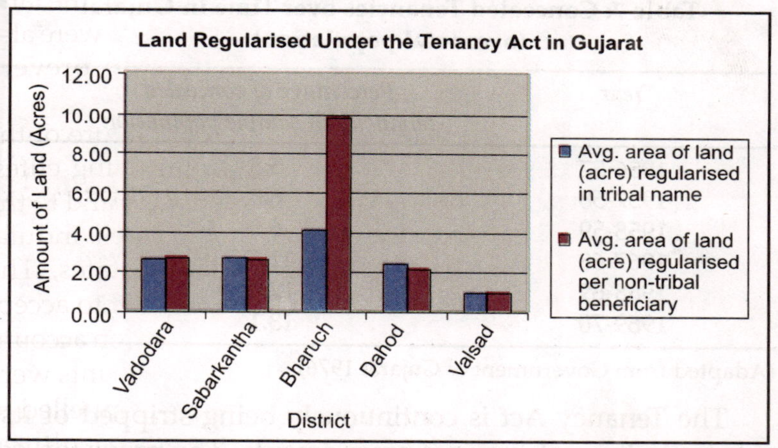

(Per individual correspondence with district collectors)

Figure 3 shows that Adivasis and non-Adivasis gained rights to nearly equivalent areas of land due to the Tenancy Act, with the exception of Bharuch in which non-Adivasi farmers gained rights to twice as much land. Given that these districts are all part of the eastern Adivasi belt (i.e. the geographical domain which was originally Adivasi land), we would expect a greater portion of land to have gone to the Adivasis, who had been relegated to working as farm labour after the settlement of non-Adivasis.

The meaning of tenancy has been manipulated on the ground. One Parsi descendent of Kodh village resided in Bombay until recently. He returned to Kodh to farm his 'ancestral land' because he believed that the expanding GIDC would have to pay him a better price for the 100 acres in his name if it was under cultivation (Judge 1999). Even after the implementation of land reforms, as many as 15% of those surveyed were absentee *khatedars* or land owners. Though the government has not collected data by social group, we see an overall pattern of concealed tenancy from 1956-57 (the year of Tiller's Day) to 1970. See data in Table 7 for details (Government of Gujarat, 1976: 28).

Table 7: Concealed Tenancies over Time in Gujarat (over total population)

Year	*Percentage of concealed tenancies in sample population*
1956-57	5.8
1957-58	6.3
1958-59	6.9
1967-68	11.3
1968-69	12.4
1969-70	13.1

(Adapted from Government of Gujarat 1976)

The Tenancy Act is continuously being stripped of its substance through various amendments. The provision of living within 8 kilometres of the land in question has been removed by an amendment in 1995. This single amendment alone is responsible for the alienation of much land because it allows for non-local large agriculturalists (and others) equipped with cash from richer economies to buy out small farmers. In 2000, the Bombay Tenancy and Agricultural Lands (Gujarat Amendment) Act was further amended by an ordinance dismissing any pending cases against violators of the 8 kilometre provision. In effect, it is as if this particular protection were erased from history. Moreover, industries do not need permission for non-agricultural activity before purchasing agricultural land, nor do they need permission of the district collector to possess such land for industrial activity (as per 63AA of Gujarat Tenancy Act which came into effect from 6th March 1977).

Removal of Intermediaries and Prevention of Fragmentation

The first legal step towards land reform was restriction of tenure to prevent alienation; the second was tenancy reform. Next came an attempt to remove land-holding intermediaries, for which several acts were passed between 1949 and 1958 by the merged Bombay State. These acts legally eliminated the tax-free tenure of petty feudal chiefs and the special land holdings and privileges granted to those who acted as tax-collecting agents in the pre-independence period. In both cases elites were not evicted from their lands, but were offered occupancy rights in exchange for appropriate payment and taxation. The *Jagirdars* (land grantees who were either kin of royalty or those granted land in exchange for royal service) retained their rights to mines and minerals and forests in the area despite laws abolishing their free-load tenancy. While this was a necessary and important official step for independent India, there were innumerable administrative problems in recording the rights of tenants who were occupying land under these intermediaries[4]. The Planning Commission report on the Implementation of Land Reforms in Gujarat (Government of India, 1966) assessed that about 130 lakh hectares was to be affected by the tenure abolition laws. Of that, 24 lakh hectares went back to the state and some 35.4 lakh hectares was distributed amongst 2.4 lakh inferior landholders. In all of Gujarat, some 51,000 people were denied the chance to become the owners of their tilled land because they did not pay the occupancy price.

Under the Bombay Prevention of Fragmentation and Consolidation of Holdings Act, 1947, sale of individual fragments of land was restricted to those who owned land in adjacent survey numbers; each block determined the size to be deemed a fragment. At the time of dividing an estate

4. See the Sabarkantha section and forest land section for examples of the problems that arose after the abolition of intermediaries

amongst heirs, a land fragment is legally indivisible. While one person would get legal title to the land, other heirs were to get their share in cash equivalent. This legislation has been very difficult to implement in Adivasi areas on the ground. It is common for the record of rights to show joint-ownership, whereas in reality a plot of land will be fissioned into as many parcels as necessary for each inheritor to manage one. Adivasi cultivators report that they do this so that each heir is given the benefit of the soil quality and agricultural productivity of each plot (so that a more productive plot does not lie solely in the hands of one nuclear family and conversely no family bears the toll of extremely poor land). Furthermore, paying out other family members is difficult given that Adivasi economies were not historically cash-based. The availability of cash for such a transaction would be limited. Studies also show that even in cases where land has been consolidated in the record of rights as per the law, in reality the land is parcelled. In 1964, a committee under H K L Kapoor was set up to determine the barriers in implementing the anti-fragmentation act, and the committee focussed on 'socially backward' areas. The circular logic of the report is typical of the state's attitude towards Adivasis: it claims that the law was needed in backward areas but cannot be implemented due to their backwardness; the law was necessary to improve the agriculture but cannot be implemented due to the poor agricultural conditions.

Gujarat Agricultural Land Ceiling Act, 1960

This legislation was based on the socialist spirit of re-distribution of wealth and took the spirit of land reform one step further. The law created a ceiling on existing holdings and on future acquisition by a cultivator, with the aim of redistribution of surplus land to the marginalised – where Adivasis were to have first preference. The ceiling itself was based on a sliding scale varying from 19 to 132 acres, according to local conditions and land quality. Broadly speaking, the ceiling area was calculated on the basis of a family earning an annual income of Rs. 1,200 in 1960. The state attempted to make strict rules preventing land transactions aimed at defeating the ceiling (such as phoney transfers amongst family members) – though those determined to evade this law succeeded through various means (see below). There are several categories of land holders that are legally exempt from this act, including approved industries; these exemptions defeat the entire purpose of the act in many ways. The lands acquired by the Gujarat state were re-distributed to private collectives and individuals on a preferential basis, giving first priority to cooperative societies with full Adivasi membership and next to individual Adivasi farmers. After Adivasis, scheduled castes were given priority.

The actual land distribution today is highly variable and is largely determined by caste and class, proof that the ceiling act failed to create an equitable distribution of agricultural land among the population of Gujarat. It is impossible, however, to directly evaluate the efficacy of the ceiling laws because no reliable data on land distribution exists. A 1966 report of the Planning Commission of Gujarat estimated that 4,562 landowners possessed a total of 2.16 lakh acres of surplus land. It is noteworthy that even official figures on the fate of that land vary very widely. Some examples are as follows.

According to the Task Force Report on Agrarian Relations, Planning Commission, Government of India, 1973 (Koshy 1974), 50,000 acres of land was declared surplus, and 25,000 acres of land was distributed in Gujarat.

A 1976 Government of Gujarat study on land reforms reports that 32,508 acres of land were declared surplus under the Agricultural Land Ceiling Act, of which the state took possession of 25,348 acres. Legal measures, such as obtaining stay orders from the Gujarat Revenue Tribunal or writ petitions in the Gujarat High Court, accounted for about 2/3 of the land area that could not be recovered by the state. The 1976 study looked at the land distribution pattern of

17,364 acres. Of that, 87% was allotted to 1,102 individual farmers. STs received 51% of the land allotted on a permanent basis. Of the land distributed on annual lease, Adivasis received 48% - thus becoming the largest number of beneficiaries of surplus land distribution on paper. However, Adivasi farmers received the least amount of land per farmer. With respect to permanent allocations, Adivasi cultivators received an average of 3.06 acres while persons from communities other than the ST, SC, other backwards classes (i.e. 'other persons') received the largest average allocation at 7.45 acres (over two times the average allocation to Adivasis). The average annual/*Eksali* lease to Adivasis was for 2.36 acres, which again was proportionately the smallest average lease size as compared to other communities. The average annual lease size to 'other backward classes' of 8.69 acres was the largest. Given the importance of the size of land holdings, we can see how the allocation of surplus land would have had only a mild impact on the status of a family of five, even if the paper promise appeared to be fulfilled (Government of Gujarat, 1976). A common technique of the landlords was to give the worst lands to the government when the ceiling was enforced. Slightly over 10% of the surplus land taken in possession was never distributed. Some 27% of this undistributed land was assessed as unfit for cultivation (Government of Gujarat, 1976).

In contrast, Harshad Trivedi reports that approximately 2.47 lakh acres of land was categorised as surplus, and the state was able to take possession of 1.49 lakh acres (about 60%). From the amount taken in possession, 80% was distributed to Adivasi farmers, scheduled castes and cooperative societies (Trivedi 1993[5]).

In 2006, the Expert Group on Prevention of Alienation of Adivasi Land and its Restoration, set up by the Ministry of

5. Though this figure was quoted in an unofficial report, Trivedi has authored and submitted a report on the same topic in 1980 for official use.

Rural Development, released a report covering the land alienation problem nationwide. Of 2,27,404 acres declared surplus, about 1,60,801 had been taken in possession. Given the total surplus of land, the amount distributed – 139,853 acres – is quite small. 13,267 Adivasi beneficiaries received 29,608 acres of land – an average of 2.23 acres per Adivasi. This stands in stark contrast to the 14,915 SC beneficiaries who received an average of 5.66 acres of land per farmer.

In Vadodara district, revenue records indicate that, after the declaration of land ceiling, 7,315 acres of land was declared surplus; of this, 5,828 acres of land was taken into possession by the government, but only 715 acres of land was distributed to Adivasi beneficiaries.

Regardless of what the exact figures were, the trend is clear. In the end, the redistribution of surplus land had little effect on marginalised people as a significant fraction was never distributed, and even that which was distributed was of poor quality and hardly arable, according to verbal reports. The records of District Collectors in the Eastern Tribal Belt support the contention that only a maximum of 50% of the surplus land was actually distributed. Under the Act, 14,000 acres of land was declared surplus and allocated strictly for Adivasis in Pardi, Umergaon, and Dharampur; of this, 9,800 acres was distributed. The Surat Deputy Collector at Vyara reports that as of 2007, a total of 575 hectares of land was declared surplus under the land ceiling law in the blocks of Nizar, Ucchal, Songadh, Vyara, Valod, Mahuva, and Bardoli. None of this land has yet been re-distributed to Adivasis. Dahod distributed a record 60% of surplus land; however, the average area taken into possession by Adivasi cultivators was quite low at 1.12 acres/farmer. A mere 418 beneficiaries who got land under land ceiling in these six districts are recorded in the Collectors' records (see Table 8).

Table 8: Distribution of Land Ceiling Surplus (in acres) Among Respondent Districts

	Vadodara	*Surat*	*Sabarkantha*	*Bharuch*	*Dahod*	*Valsad*
Percentage of surplus land distributed to Adivasis	13.04	0	10.76	16.26	60.76	32.89
Avg. area of land (acres) redistributed to Adivasis from ceiling surplus	3.31	none distributed	2.61	3.13	1.12	1.66

(Per individual correspondence with District Collectors)

Failure of land reforms

The case study data shows that Adivasi land alienation is a result of the failure of governance, which in turn results from structural defects in the notion of the state and state responsibility towards the people. Overall there existed a nexus between state laws, the bureaucracy, and private actors that resulted in botched land reforms. Encounters with the modern state and alien ways promoted an inferiority complex amongst Adivasis that reinforced the ability of non-Adivasis to exploit them, and rendered Adivasis compliant with many legal processes that had a negative impact on them. Even today, 71% of the rural Adivasi population is illiterate. Illiteracy also made Adivasis easy victims of the upper-castes, as Adivasis could be disenfranchised of their rights without their knowledge.

Paramjit Judge (1999) argues that the positive benefits of land reforms in Gujarat are paper artefacts. Based on a micro-study of Khodh village in Bharuch District, Judge (1999) discusses the following issues at the village level that aggravated the land problem in Adivasi Gujarat. In the absence of an honest and functioning administration, nepotism and cronyism prevails. The first allegiance of officials is to their own caste/religious community. Even if an Adivasi wins in one court, he may not win the overall battle given the various appellate authorities. The non-Adivasi is usually more in a position to fight extended legal battles. Land that is acquired and allotted to Adivasis under the land ceiling acts has often been of poor quality. Without financial assistance for improvement, certain lands essentially lie fallow. The village level bureaucracy (i.e. the *talatis*) favour the land-owning class, and take decisions in their interest. This might be in the timing of allocation (e.g. give a yearly lease when the sowing season is nearly over) or in allowing access to farmland as pastures to the upper classes. The debt cycle is perpetuated by the land owners, who lend money and collect interest in such a manner that all the debtor's earnings are exhausted in repaying the debt. This often leads to permanent land alienation and bonded labour. The power of owning land translates into political power (i.e. being elected as the *sarpanch*, or holding the position of the police *patel*), and political power feeds back into the maintenance of land ownership. The impact of failed development schemes also keeps people in debt. For example, in drought conditions, Adivasis cannot manage to feed the milch cattle which they have purchased through loans. As a result, they cannot sell milk to the dairy, and remain in debt for the cattle (Judge 1999).

2.3 Class-based Exploitation and Land Alienation

Historical Narrative of Dispossession by Private Hands

The legal provisions against alienation of private lands have been discussed in the previous section on land reforms. This section presents some examples and narratives of how such alienation took place.

A good first example is the fate of Adivasi lands in Valia Block of the Rajpipla Princely State. The *Raasti*, or 'civilised non-Adivasi', villages in the western corner of the block were first surveyed and settled between 1885 and 1890. The

Adivasis in interior Valia believe that their predecessors had occupied the fertile western corner of Valia first, but then lost it to non-Adivasis. Some resisted the conquest by moving further interior into the jungle and so on; others remained to work as agricultural labourers in the fields of non-Adivasis (these were known as *chakars*, and the first Settlement Report recorded over 4,000 such labourers). The original settlement report of this area noted that many land transfers circumvented standard procedure and were not recorded in the revenue records. Small land-holdings were particularly prone to this (Pinto, not dated).

Before the first survey settlement (1892), all of the land in Bhamadia village of Valia block was controlled by the Bhil headman (or Vahavo). Families cultivated together, divided up the produce among households, and the headman regulated who would cultivate what area. Revenue in the form of farm produce was collected from the headman. Hunting, forest foraging, and sale of forest timber were sources of supplemental nutrition and income. However, by the time survey settlement was completed in 1896, all uncultivated land was declared government fallow land and the powers of the headman to freely allot forest land for cultivation were curtailed (Pinto, not dated).

Table 9: Land Ownership and Classification in Bhamadia Village After the Initial Settlement

Year	*Land owned by Adivasis (acres)*	*Land owned by non-Adivasis (acres)*	*Uncultivated government land (acres)*	*Non-agricultural Land (acres)*	*Wasteland (acres)*
1909	591.28	67.12	102.07	39.28	31.1
1928	602	153.2	5.13	39.3	31.1
1957	130	631.6	—	—	—

(Pinto not dated)

There is historical proof that some of those ousted from the fertile western corner settled in Bhamadia. Bhamadia village was occupied totally by Adivasis according to the first surveys. However, by 1909, 11% of cultivated lands in the village were in the name of non-Adivasis. By 1928, 18% of the land was in the control of non-Adivasis (see Table 9 and Figure 4). Pinto's survey of 108 landowners in Bhamadia revealed that only 66% of them are residents of the village. The absentee landlords come from the Rajput, Patidar, Parsi and Adivasi communities, and 19% of them now live in the USA. Together, the absentee land lords own over half the land. Nearly 60% of the land is with only 5.3% of the population, who manage holdings 15 acres and above. Amongst these large land holders (as classified by the Bharuch District Rural Development Agency), 54.5% are Adivasis. In contrast, 115 Adivasi household officially own no land (Pinto, not dated).

Figure 4: Land Ownership in Bhamadia Village Over Time

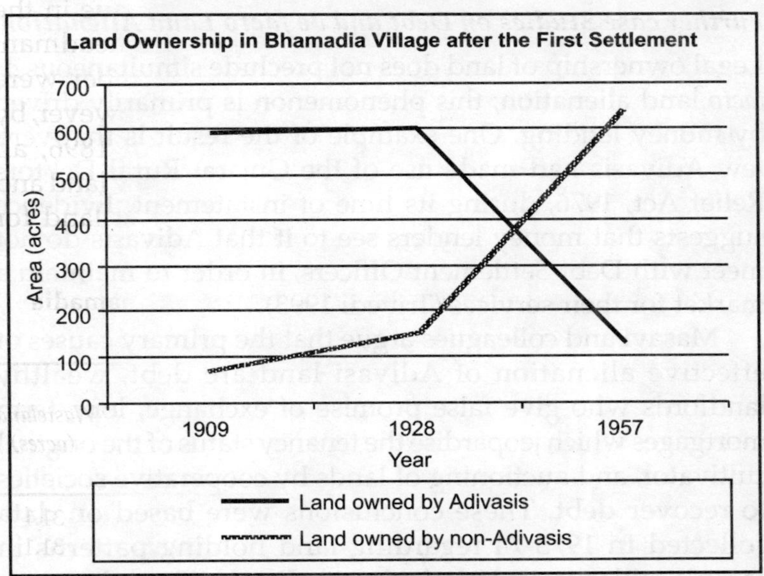

(Pinto not dated)

The Adivasis of Bhamadia state that large amounts of land were mortgaged to Bania money lenders, who then in turn sold the lands to Rajputs and Patidars. The most fertile lands were transferred to non-Adivasis through this process. Adivasis do not remember this process as a consensual sale of their lands; rather, even the language used reflects that they feel that their lands were unfairly swallowed up by powerful castes hailing from the plains. Elders from the village remember that the decades leading up to independence were poor agriculturally (famine in the 1930s and so on), and forced many to mortgage their lands at a pittance. Moneylenders conspired with police to physically beat Adivasi farmers into signing away their lands. The very few Adivasis who adopted formal education were in a position to access land through the Land to the Tillers legislations. Generally, there was a sense among the villagers that tenancy reforms could only be successful in the areas where absentee landlords were completely out of the picture.

Further case Studies on Debt and de facto Land Alienation

Legal ownership of land does not preclude simultaneous *de facto* land alienation; this phenomenon is primarily driven by money lending. One example of the result is that very few Adivasis had made use of the Gujarat Rural Debtors Relief Act, 1976, during its time of instatement. Evidence suggests that money lenders see to it that Adivasis do not meet with Debt Settlement Officers, in order to maintain a market for their services (Trivedi 1993).

Masavi and colleagues argue that the primary causes of effective alienation of Adivasi land are debt, wealthy landlords who give false promise of exchange, long-term mortgages which jeopardise the tenancy status of the original cultivator, and auctioning of lands by cooperative societies to recover debt. These conclusions were based on data collected in 1973-74 regarding land holding patterns in sample villages in Valod (Surat), Danta (Banaskantha), Chhotaudepur (Vadodara), and Jhalod (Panchmahals) blocks. The researchers focused on villages that were predominantly Adivasi, but have had long term contact with non-Adivasis and were connected to the outside world by road. Over two hundred land owners (khatedars) were covered.

Table 10: Cross-village Glimpse of Debt

Taluka	*Danta*	*Valod*	*Chhotaudepur*	*Jhalod*
Geographical location in state	North	South	South	North
Adivasi population	Bhil	70% Choudary; also Dhodia, Gamit, Dubla, Konkna, and Kotwalia	Mostly Rathwas, Bhils, Tadvis, and Naiks	Bhils and Patelias
Main crop	Maize	Jowar, paddy, gram	maize and jowar	maize, some wheat
Cash crop cultivated	cotton and groundnut	cotton, sugarcane	cotton and groundnut	none
Over 35% forest	yes	no	no	yes
Over 20% non agricultural land	yes	no	no	no
Percentage area under irrigation	11.1	0.7	12.7	11.4
Percentage of land owners with less than 5 acres	51.2	48.1	16.7	7.9
Most frequent reason for borrowing money	Household expense	Agricultural Expense	Household expense	Household expense
Percentage of borrowing from moneylenders	63.5	54.8	62.2	47.2
Most frequent debt bracket (in Rs)	0-50	51-100	above 500	51-100
Percentage of owners mortgaging land to total land owners	39	27.3	31.2	37.4
Percentage of mortgages to other Adivasi cultivators	25	77.8	40	100

(Masavi et al. not dated)

Masavi and colleagues observed that moneylenders were not interested in claiming the land as their own, due to legal obstacles. Moneylenders' interest was in seizing the standing crop, which in effect led to indentured servitude. According to Masavi *et al.*, 68% of borrowings happened within the community. The degree of the problem as shown in Table 10 is striking, despite the variation in Adivasi communities, extent of cash indebtedness and geographical position, an average of one third of Adivasi land owners have mortgaged their lands. Of course, where possible, the money lending class did manipulate village records in order to gain ownership of lands before the enactment of the Bombay Tenancy Act. There were also cases of land transfers where the Adivasi *khatedars* were totally unaware of the transfer (the land was being farmed by others the whole time).

Kodh village, Valia block in Bharuch district, has a mixed Bhil Vasava and Muslim population, with some Parsis and Patels. The Bhil elders recalled that before a powerful Parsi family migrated to the area in the early 1900s, the entire village community engaged in subsistence agriculture. This Parsi family, headed by a man named Burorji, distilled liquor which he sold on credit, thus beginning money-lending. Unable to keep written records, the non-literate Adivasis gave their thumb prints on sale documents and mortgage documents indiscriminately. Through such activities, the Burorji family acquired 1,000 acres of land. This anecdote sufficiently captures the reality of many Adivasi communities of the area (Judge 1999).

Chandrawan (Netrang, Bharuch) is an entirely Adivasi village. In Chandrawan, a single Parsi family controls lands that were allotted in the names of at least 4 different farming families. This family has also undergone a divorce – only in name – in order to maintain rights over a larger area of land, and act as if the divorce is genuine whenever officials come to visit (Judge 1999).

Judge presents anecdotal evidence from another village, Kesargam, in Valia block. Though this village has an Adivasi majority and 440 ha of culturable land, only 5 of 42 ST families own land. Despite being in a slim minority, caste Patels wield power and influence to hang on to their lands. There is a case where revenue was never paid, yet land was allotted. Another case involves a landowner paying revenue on land declared surplus in order to maintain rights over it (Judge 1999).

The commodification of land and resource scarcity has led to greater internal stratification among Adivasis. Revenue land remains a complex and sensitive issue. In Sagtala village of Devgadh Baria, Dahod, descendants of the original Naik settlers of the village hardly possess any land today. They claim that for some years, the preceding generation worked as police for the King, and thus were absent from the village on and off. In that period, other Naik residents of the village had that land surveyed as *Khalsa*. That land was then regularised in the name of other Naik residents, who claimed to have been cultivating it. This land is thus under dispute. Generally in Devgadh Baria land holdings are extremely small and internal disputes amongst Adivasis over land are not uncommon. Adivasis have encroached on common property lands by providing evidence sufficient to register a particular plot of land as *khalsa* and then cultivate it (sometimes using force to prevent other Adivasis from doing the same), in order to eventually claim it under the provisions of the tenancy act.

Most Adivasi land alienation in Surat district took place before 1961, when the notification to protect tenure took effect. In the 1980s there was a lack of consciousness over land/property rights, and therefore hardly any Adivasi farmers approached *Talatis* for records of their rights. Those that did were usually met with resistance and reluctance. Of those surveyed in Surat, 5.2% reported experiencing land alienation first hand (Jani and Ganguly 2000). This rate is relatively lower than the central and northern districts surveyed, and roughly the same as that of Panchmahal.

Adivasis today report that the *Kisan* (farmer) movement

of Surat, which began in 1932 under the banner of the socialist *Kisan Sabha* (led by Indulal Yagnik), is still alive today. In Mandvi block of Surat District, it is well known that Parsi traders strategically brought non-literate Vasavas and Chaudharies into debt to later take over the lands of the indebted. During the Land to the Tiller Reforms, about 50% of the land was given back to Adivasis on paper. In one case, a single Parsi landlord had taken possession of about 40 acres belonging to 31 families. While 26 of these families were able to get possession, there are 16 families who are still fighting a case in the High Court to have these lands properly surveyed so that they may take possession. However, it is very difficult for the Adivasis to actually attend court, and the case still drags on.

In Valsad, the incidence of land alienation was found to be 4.0 % in three sample villages (Jani and Ganguly 2000). This was the lowest rate of alienation detected amongst the sampled Adivasi districts. Tenancy reforms seem to have had a positive impact on some groups of Adivasis in Valsad Block. In Umergaon block, occupancy was granted to 19,423 tenants, who were given 46,426 acres of land. The Dublas are mostly landless labourers in Gujarat. However, in Umergaon, because of tenancy reform implementation and the land ceiling, the Halpati group of the Dublas have become part of the land holding Adivasis in this district. In Dharampur block, mostly the Kukna tribe are land holders.

The average incidence of land alienation in three villages of Sabarkantha was found to be 10.3% (Jani and Ganguly 2000). The farmers of this district have had problems with land alienation due to mortgage. The original lands of Adivasis remain dispossessed due to upper-caste political clout and also long standing loyalty to the non-Adivasis involved. Problems of concealed tenancy are rampant here. Many Adivasi cultivators had lost possession of their land before Bombay Tenancy Act due to voluntary surrenders of land, temporary disuse of land, or legal action taken by the landlord declaring that the Adivasi was not a tenant of the land. As a result of the Bombay Tenancy Act, about 1,019 Adivasis got rights over 2,754 hectares of land[6], while 12,253 non-Adivasis got about 31,579 hectares of land. Under land ceiling, only about 11% of what was declared surplus land was actually distributed to Adivasi farmers; 97 individuals and one cooperative received the land[7]. As of 1980 there were 1,504 documented cases of land alienation in Khedbrahma, Meghraj, Bhiloda, and Vijaynagar blocks. Only 57 of these cases were between Adivasis and non-Adivasis; 96% of the cases of land alienation were the result of Adivasi land sales to other Adivasis; none were sanctioned by the Collector (Trivedi 1993). The district however did distribute waste land to Adivasis since 1960s, distributing a maximum of 461 hectares amongst 657 individuals between 1981 and 1990. The district acknowledges acquisition of about 573 hectares from 313 families under the Land Acquisition Act. About 3,431 hectares of land has been converted from new tenure to old tenure in this district since the 1990s.

In a region of Panchmahals, formerly part of the Sant princely state, the ruler, Pushpa Singh, divided his land amongst his adult sons to avoid losing it due to the abolition of intermediaries. However, some of his tenants did get possession of the lands they were tilling. Many tenants were threatened and chased off the land before they could claim rights to it. On paper, there were no tenants though in reality the entire area was being cultivated by labourers (Judge 1999).

Contemporary incidence of land alienation in Panchmahal was found to be 8.3% in a sample survey of 3 villages (Jani and Ganguly 2000). Trivedi reports 900 cases of Adivasi cultivators who acted as farm labourers to money-lenders or effectively became servant-farmers of their own lands due to heavy debts. This is also a district with heavy migration, leading to the neglect of agriculture, which itself

6. Per correspondence with the District Collector of Sabarkantha under the RTI act
7. ibid.

heightens the chances of land alienation. As of 1993, 3,046 cases had been filed to restore possession of alienated land under Section 73A – 2,523 cases were disposed of, and in 757 cases the courts ordered that the land be restored to the Adivasi farmers, but these had not been restored at the time of the study. Typical of Adivasi land holdings, there were cases where even four generations had passed, but divisions of land had not been recorded in the village books (Trivedi 1993). This creates an inaccurate picture of the pressure on land, and such farmers have no possibility of getting a loan against their land assets, as there is no official record. Trivedi reports that out of 6,000 cases of land transfer, Adivasis themselves refused to take possession of their own land in 1,400. This, he claims, reflects the impact of a severe social hierarchy and historical system of exploitation that has penetrated the very psychology of an entire society.

Pardi Satyagraha

As in many places in South Gujarat, the Adivasis were the original owners of land in Pardi, but land reforms and the predatory lending practices of communities migrating to the area led to the loss of Adivasi lands. This set the stage for a 15-year long struggle over the grasslands controlled by high caste Hindus and Parsis in Pardi block of Valsad district. One-hundred landlords controlled 75% of the total cultivatable land in Pardi block in 1952. These landlords were more interested in the business of growing grass to sell to the lucrative Bombay fodder trade than in growing food crops. The Adivasis, already ousted from their lands and rendered landless, could hardly earn a living working on grass fields, as little labour is required for such cultivation. Their cattle also were banned from feeding on the grasslands, though these lands had in fact been owned by them (Desai 2002).

Ishwarbhai Desai, a socialist, envisioned a Gandhian *Satyagraha* to arrive at justice for the Adivasis. The *satyagraha* would aim at addressing two distinct problems: 1) the cultivation of grass on land suitable for food crops thwarts the Adivasi labourers' possibility of finding work and jeopardizes the supply of grain in order to increase profits to the landlord; and 2) Adivasi tenancy and the lack of recognition of their rights. The movement was led by the *Kisan Panchayat*, and sought to grow food crops on the grasslands. The *Satyagraha* commenced on 1st September 1953. An 80-year old Adivasi woman and a well known socialist, Ashok Mehta, trespassed and tilled the land of a landlord with 3,000 acres of land in the village of Dumlav. About 1,050 satyagrahis – nearly 1/10 women – pledged non-violence and engaged in the struggle. Both the landlord lobby and the Congress Party sought the defeat of the *Satyagrahis*; mass arrests and other methods were used to suppress the movement. However, the non-violent fight continued for fifteen long years. The final agreement between the landlords, the state, and the *Satyagrahis* was reached in 1967, and involved the landlords handing over of 14,000 acres of land to the state for redistribution to indigent farmers. Of the 14,000 acres, 6,000 acres were in any case surplus lands as per the Land Ceiling Act, and 8,000 acres were surrendered voluntarily (Desai 2002).

This is yet another case that highlights the role of state collusion in the inequitable distribution of land in Adivasi areas. Even though the law was on the side of the people, the administration was not. In addition to the ceiling provisions, Section 65 of the BLRC expressly allows for the acquisition for private grasslands for the cultivation of food crops. If the government had fulfilled its duty to the public, this protracted *satyagraha* might have been avoided.

Long Range Effects of Alienation

Cash poverty and few material assets place the Adivasis of Panchmahals in a vicious cycle of debt and land deficit. Food security is a major issue. This in turn affects labour migration, increases bride price, and results in increased liquor consumption, which in turn affect land holding patterns. Small land holdings characterize Adivasi agriculture in this

Table 11: Cultivators, Labourers, and Rural Workers per Hectare by Taluka (2001 Census)

Taluka	*District*	*Total workers*	*Cultivators*			*Agricultural Labourers*		
		Absolute	*Absolute*	*% to Total Workers*	*Per 100 Hectares*	*Absolute*	*% to Total Workers*	*Per 100 Hectares*
Palanpur	Banaskantha	103122.0	30717.0	29.8	50.8	21653.0	21.0	35.8
Danta	Banaskantha	70997.0	31791.0	44.8	154.3	19252.0	27.1	93.4
Bhiloda	Sabarkantha	86042.0	36803.0	42.8	96.7	27162.0	31.6	71.4
Meghraj	Sabarkantha	65903.0	39483.0	59.9	113.6	16325.0	24.8	47.0
Khedbrahma	Sabarkantha	94770.0	43728.0	46.1	137.3	36074.0	38.1	113.3
Vijanagar	Sabarkantha	37278.0	17450.0	46.8	151.7	12160.0	32.6	105.7
Santrampur	Panchmahal	102346.0	62366.0	60.9	208.9	28269.0	27.6	94.7
Devgadhbaria	Dahod	109075.0	76446.0	70.1	236.6	13596.0	12.5	42.1
Limkheda	Dahod	120784.0	85151.0	70.5	289.5	17447.0	14.4	59.3
Jhalod	Dahod	168341.0	110135.0	65.4	223.1	43105.0	25.6	87.3
Dahod	Dahod	126728.0	60398.0	47.7	175.0	42996.0	33.9	124.6
Halol	Dahod	75081.0	32025.0	42.7	102.3	26365.0	35.1	84.2
Godhra	Dahod	129727.0	73422.0	56.6	164.5	33160.0	25.6	74.3
Chhotaudepur	Vadodara	93113.0	41742.0	44.8	122.8	40463.0	43.5	119.0
Pavi Jetpur	Vadodara	128978.0	67978.0	52.7	133.6	48364.0	37.5	95.1
Naswadi	Vadodara	68992.0	22311.0	32.3	72.8	40847.0	59.2	133.4
Tilakwada	Narmada	30133.0	9970.0	33.1	52.4	15080.0	50.0	79.3
Sankheda	Vadodara	91432.0	29311.0	32.1	54.3	46959.0	51.4	87.0
Jhagadia	Bharuch	84279.0	16196.0	19.2	34.5	45733.0	54.3	97.3
Valia	Bharuch	65884.0	12152.0	18.4	30.3	40085.0	60.8	99.9
Ankleshwar	Bharuch	58628.0	8221.0	14.0	25.4	23814.0	40.6	73.6

Sagbara	Narmada	46589.0	15784.0	33.9	96.1	23790.0	51.1	144.8
Nandod	Narmada	89651.0	26214.0	29.2	54.3	44583.0	49.7	92.4
Dediapada	Narmada	76882.0	34433.0	44.8	129.2	33720.0	43.9	126.5
Vyara	Surat	123965.0	58144.0	46.9	122.2	40062.0	32.3	84.2
Valod	Surat	46564.0	10156.0	21.8	61.8	23146.0	49.7	140.9
Songadh	Surat	99175.0	44983.0	45.4	106.2	32757.0	33.0	77.3
Uchchhal	Surat	44801.0	13393.0	29.9	161.4	25065.0	55.9	302.0
Nizar	Surat	58374.0	13449.0	23.0	63.7	35930.0	61.6	170.2
Mahuva	Surat	80979.0	20757.0	25.6	77.9	40212.0	49.7	150.9
Mandvi	Surat	99614.0	31526.0	31.6	78.7	41443.0	41.6	103.4
Mangrol	Surat	58740.0	30140.0	51.3	71.8	19023.0	32.4	45.3
Bardoli	Surat	79372.0	8218.0	10.4	27.8	50022.0	63.0	168.9
Chikhli	Navsari	145839.0	53233.0	36.5	109.8	60406.0	41.4	124.6
Pardi	Valsad	117613.0	30410.0	25.9	86.8	30472.0	25.9	87.0
Umbergaon	Valsad	87476.0	15053.0	17.2	61.3	21151.0	24.2	86.1
Dharampur	Valsad	89478.0	46111.0	51.5	189.1	29082.0	32.5	119.2
Vansda	Navsari	109926.0	55120.0	50.1	200.6	32807.0	29.8	119.4
Dangs	Dangs	92905.0	53356.0	57.4	96.5	26582.0	28.6	48.1
		3459576.0	1468276.0	40.1	113.5	1249162.0	38.3	102.8

area. Land alienation is common yet has is rarely recorded. Dahod district now has the highest average density of cultivators in the state – 243 cultivators per 100 hectares, as compared to the state average of 63 cultivators per 100 hectares. The relatively lower proportion of agricultural labourers (see Table 11) is also a result of the poor quality of land in the area, which is not conducive to growing cash-crops on a large scale.

Migration patterns in Panchmahals and Dahod are useful to understanding how land holding patterns have broader impacts on the society and culture of indigenous communities. In the 1940s, the Bhils of Panchmahal relied on agriculture for 60-70% of their income (Naik 1956). By the 1990s, only about 12% of Bhil households were able to meet their food needs through agriculture alone. Iyengar (undated) charges that government interventions into the area failed because of poor long-term planning and bad internal design. Iyengar also charges that the quality of land is so poor that ultimately there is no incentive to work it. He argues that small Adivasi farmers lost out to those with large land holdings who were the biggest beneficiaries of government schemes. Almost all Adivasis of Panchmahal own land, yet migration is rampant. The restriction on traditional use and sale of forest goods and the drying up of opportunities in public works compels Bhils to go further in search of work. In the next few years we must see how the much awaited national rural employment guarantee act will impact this chain of events. Mosse and colleagues (2000) surveyed 8 villages in Panchmahal district covering 784 households, of which 496 had migrants – revealing that 63% of households migrated. An average of 2.8 people per household migrated for an average of 5.8 months each. Mosse *et al.* found that seasonal labour migration is increasing in the sample villages in the Panchmahals, and that women made up 87% of the increase. Bhils typically perform unskilled labour tasks. Construction contractors are one of the main employers, and those from Panchmahals tend to go to Vadodara (although

Surat and Ahmedabad are also important targets for Adivasi migrant labour in Gujarat). This influences the scenario of small farming at home, since there is little labour input to improve agriculture outputs in the village. This leads to a downward spiral in which poor land quality leads to migration and migration leads to further deterioration of agricultural outputs.

2.4 Forest Law

A Dangi Adivasi responded to official questioning regarding proof of his claim to forest land by saying '[The] very fact that I am alive and before you, Sir, is the proof' (Engineer 2002: 313). The symbiotic association between Adivasis and the forests is well known; Adivasi existence depends on forests, while forests tend to exist today primarily where Adivasis have maintained them. However this inference is rarely taken to its logical conclusion, and both the state administration and public have been reluctant to grant Adivasis rights to the land that they have occupied, used and protected for generations. To date, the Adivasis of Gujarat have suffered from the passive and active violence of the forest department, as well as coped with administrative inaction and detrimental state policies. The Forest Department has historically undertaken a program of encroachment onto cultivated land to expand the area under their control, while forest resources accessible to Adivasis are continually shrinking. The struggle to restore historical rights over forest land and resources to the people has been legally won on paper at the central level, yet the successful implementation of the resulting legislation is awaited.

The area of land under the Forest Department changed at the time of the formation of the State of Gujarat. While some forest land was denotified to settle people in the Dangs, significant portions of Bharuch and Sabarkantha districts came under the Forest Department's control during that time (see Table 12). After state formation, the Gujarat Forest Department managed to increase the area under its control by almost 4 lakh hectares, largely by acquiring private forests and taking over areas classified as government wastelands. Currently, about 19.11 lakh hectares of land are under its control. Of the total forest area in Gujarat, 14.15 lakh hectares of Gujarat's forest is classified as reserved, 39,485 hectares as protected, and over 4.5 lakh hectares are unclassified (Gujarat Forest Statistics, 2003). In reality, the actual forest cover of Gujarat is only 15.15 lakh hectares, and represents 7.7% of the total geographic area of the state (Forest Survey of India, 2001). This forest cover is spread in 4,732 villages with a total population of about 3.18 million (Xavier 2007).

Table 12: District-level Changes in Forest Land between 1956-61

	1956-57, (acres)	*1960-61, (acres)*	*Absolute Change (acres)*
Sabarkantha	180,300	212,900	32,600
Ahmedabad	2,200	n/a	n/a
Kheda/Nadiad	21,000	28,700	7,700
Panchmahals	396,900	388,400	– 8,500
Vadodara	126,300	138,100	11,800
Bharuch	217,600	258,600	41,000
Surat	325,100	338,400	13,300
Dangs	352,100	288,000	– 64,100
Banaskantha	210,300	209,900	– 400
Total	1,831,800	1,863,000	31,200

Census of India. Note that 1971 data is available and was collected by block, however changing administrative boundaries lessen its reference value

About 44% of the area under the control of the Forest Department in Gujarat is in 31 blocks where 79% of Gujarat's Adivasi population resides (in which, on average, Adivasis make up two-thirds of the population). The Forest Department controls up to 57% of the land in some blocks, and up to 80% in some of the Revenue villages (data not shown). See Table 13 for block-wise data on forest land and ST population distribution in Gujarat.

Table 13: Forest Land and ST Population in Scheduled Blocks

Taluka	*District*	*Total area (in hectares)*	*Total Forest Land (in Hectares)*	*Percentage of forest over total area*	*Total ST population*	*Percentage ST population in Taluka*
Palanpur	Banaskantha	144228.2	39284	27.2	47639	12.0
Danta	Banaskantha	84333.56	46367.48	55.0	64302	48.9
Bhiloda	Sabarkantha	72045.35	20373.6	28.3	93858	53.5
Meghraj	Sabarkantha	53914.5	9405.69	17.4	43407	37.9
Khedbrahma	Sabarkantha	80807.03	31299.93	38.7	104232	62.7
Vijaynagar	Sabarkantha	45605.11	26252.95	57.6	53868	73.4
Santrampur	Panchmahal	135435.1	36077.67	26.6	330594	79.2
Devgadhbaria	(Panchmahal)	113443.2	28634.28	25.2	127817	37.5
Limkheda	(Panchmahal)	106357.2	35533.8	33.4	178601	62.2
Jhalod	(Panchmahal)	79839.79	14220.8	17.8	242163	87.8
Dahod	(Panchmahal)	84330.55	15767.18	18.7	309793	77.2
Halol	(Panchmahal)	48116.72	9290.56	19.3	46186	28.6
Godhra	(Panchmahal)	99903.88	19540.1	19.6	88000	20.9
Chhotaudepur	Vadodara	136716.9	42608.95	31.2	269642	88.6
Pavi Jetpur	Vadodara	80123.02	7885.44	9.8	163193	81.7
Naswadi	Vadodara	53516.56	15981.7	29.9	90825	84.5
Tilakwada	(Vadodara)	24441.64	1023.93	4.2	26089	50.7
Sankheda	Vadodara	69595.92	2738.56	3.9	68412	41.3

Jhagadia	Bharuch	80835.49	15346.56	19.0	99536	65.8
Valia	Bharuch	51402.64	2664.87	5.2	88973	76.5
Ankleshwar	Bharuch	42022.04	91.05	0.2	58382	30.7
Sagbara	Narmada	36368.28	12215.71	33.6	67956	91.1
Nandod	Narmada	110895.4	35775.84	32.3	139234	66.7
Dediapada	Narmada	102386.6	59312.16	57.9	109042	95.1
Vyara	(Surat)	80457.36	21960.72	27.3	190017	86.9
Valod	(Surat)	20226.13	104.2	0.5	57134	74.2
Songadh	(Surat)	119161.2	32699.48	27.4	142684	82.5
Uchchhal	(Surat)	62150.77	22836.48	36.7	62194	97.7
Nizar	(Surat)	39590.48	124.93	0.3	74044	78.2
Mahuva	Surat	35401.04	2728.91	7.7	100491	79.7
Mandvi	Surat	72346.01	18395.13	25.4	124751	77.3
Mangrol	Surat	82839.1	11057.63	13.3	128115	65.1
Bardoli	Surat	36886.86	0	0.0	91501	51.2
Chikhli	(Valsad)	57352.37	1169.35	2.0	183020	70.2
Pardi	Valsad	39567.66	344.11	0.9	139165	51.1
Umbergaon	Valsad	34836.12	4293.23	12.3	97929	53.9
Dharampur	Valsad	163431.5	88765.52	54.3	288728	94.9
Vansda	(Valsad)	59345.99	21638.56	36.5	156632	90.1
Dangs	Dangs	171723.2	91210.58	53.1	135386	94.0

Census of India, 1991. Parentheses indicate district change after the point of data collection; district shown is based on 1991 data.

There are one national park and six wildlife sanctuaries in the Eastern Adivasi belt of Gujarat totalling 1.7 lakh hectares. Though the rights of Adivasis are restricted in these areas under the Wild Life (Protection) Act, there has not been a systematic effort to displace or relocate people from the sanctuaries where Adivasi communities reside. See the Table 14 for a listing.

Table 14: National Parks and Wildlife Sanctuaries in the Eastern Adivasi Belt of Gujarat

Name	*Year of establish-ment*	*Area (sq. km)*	*Location*
Vansda National Park	1979	23.99	Vansda, Navsari District
Purna Wildlife Sanctuary	1990	160.84	Dangs District
Jambughoda Sanctuary	1990	130.38	Jambughoda, Panchmahal District
Shoolpanshwar Sanctuary	1982	607.70	Narmada District
Ratanmahal Sanctuary	1982	55.65	Ratanmahal, Dahod District
Jessore Sloth Bear Sanctuary	1978	180.66	Jessore Hills, District Banaskantha
Balaram Ambaji Sanctuary	1989	542.08	Banaskantha District

(http://gujaratforest.gov.in)

In sample villages throughout Gujarat state, Iyengar found that the present day tree population is a mere 1-15% of what it was thirty years ago (Iyengar 2002). Two groups of people were mainly responsible for this deforestation:

1. The *Jagirdars*. Even after the official abolition of *Jagirdari* in1953, *Jagirdars* remained in control of most of the forest and used legal avenues to hold on to what they had. In reaction to the threat of losing the forest as a result of the enactment of the Gujarat Private Forests (Acquisition) Act, 1972, the *Jagirdars* sought to extract maximum profit from their forests before restrictions came into force, and conducted massive tree-felling.

2. The Forest Department. From the 1960s to early 1980s, the forest department engaged in massive and systematic contract cutting of forests.

Despite this, it is the Adivasis who have suffered the most under the oppressive restrictions of the forest laws.

Forest Villages

Moreover, the British also managed to use the Adivasis themselves– the historical protectors of the forest – as the foot soldiers for its destruction. The British created a system of Forest Villages in Gujarat as in other states in order to ensure a steady supply of labour to harvest forest goods for profit, as well as labour to extinguish the occasional forest fire. These 'villages' were actually settlements created by the Forest Department in which they housed Adivasi migrant workers who were used to harvest timber. Forest Villages remained outside the purview of the Revenue Department and Adivasis settled there have never had real ownership rights over land. Instead, they have been granted temporary, yet theoretically perpetual, leases over forest lands, which they were allowed to clear and cultivate. There are 115 such Forest Villages throughout Gujarat. There are also 79 cases of Revenue Villages with forest land where Adivasis were encouraged to settle because of the labour they could provide. The Adivasis involved in this latter case would be entitled to ownership over land and various development schemes offered by the Revenue Department. See Table 15 for details. (Prasad and Jahagirdar 1993).

Certain norms regarding the interaction of the settlers and the Forest Department existed (apparently not a formal contract). These norms included: 1) the settlers must be available to provide labour at the behest of forest officers and 2) the settlers must voluntarily partake in forest tending. By convention, the settlers were provided land for cultivation and housing, rights to collect fuel wood, grazing rights, and rights to collect minor forest produce for consumption and sale (Prasad and Jahagirdar 1993).

Table 15: Forest Settlement Villages and Revenue Villages with Forest Settlers in Gujarat

Forest Circle	*Forest Division*	*No. of Forest Villages*	*Area cultivated (Ha)*	*Families*
Surat	Vyara	13	397.52	99
	Rajpipla (E)	32	1355.16	578
	Rajpipla (W)	103	3373.52	1292
Vadodara	Baria	11	575.56	262
	Godhra	11	604.19	467
	Chotaudepur	9	293.08	182
Junagadh	Gir (E)	5	716.74	105
	Gir (W)	9	1142.18	217
	Junagadh	1	62.09	30
	Total	**194**	**8520.04**	**3232**

Note: This includes the number of Khatedars and not families who do not cultivate. (Prasad and Jahagirdar 1993)

The residents of forest villages, traditionally disadvantaged lacking land ownership, are denied agricultural loans. There is no panchayat or local governance system, and most Revenue Department development schemes are not implemented. In recent years, there have been some positive interventions by the Forest Department aimed although at reducing the 'burden' of these communities on the forest. For example, solar lantern schemes and the distribution of bricks and cement to build *pucca* homes introduced in some forest villages which although hardly compensates for the lack of grid electricity as well as the absence of other facilities, and most importantly, security of land tenure. Furthermore, in the contemporary era of development-induced displacement, residents of Forest Settlement Villages lose out since they are not compensated for their land loss (Lobo and Kumar 2007).

Lack of Recognition of Rights

Adivasis residing in revenue villages and reliant on forest land are not without their problems. The administration never conducted any proper survey and settlement of the rights of occupants of lands notified as forest lands, and has never faithfully implemented the numerous state legislations that allow for granting legal entitlements of land (see Box 1 for a timeline of Gujarat Forest law). The process of settling rights of forest dwellers according to the legal provisions of the Indian Forest Act 1927 was never conducted by the Forest Settlement Officers, and this was particularly true in remote regions. Similarly, provisions of the Wildlife Protection Act, 1972 dictating the settlement procedure were never followed. For example, in Dediapada block of Narmada District, Section 4 notices under the IFA[8] were served in 1965,and the Forest Department took control of the majority of the block's by 1975 (including the large areas occupied by Adivasi cultivators) without ever having done the required survey (Campaign for survival and Dignity 2003).

Box 1: Timeline for Gujarat related forest laws

5th July 1972

A Gujarat GR guaranteed that up to 8 acres of forest land cultivations prior to 31st December 1967 would be regularised.

12th February 1992 (and 19th February 1992)

Committee formed to implement the Central circulars (13-1-80 FP issued on 18th September 1990 and no. 13-1-91 FP dated 26th August 1991), which were designed to address the problem of illegal encroachments. The Committee was to take on a dialog with representatives of the people.

6th October 1992

This GR stated that for Adivasis and other backwards people conducting unauthorised farming in forest areas, land would be regularised under the following conditions: 1) land had been farmed before 1980 and Forest Department has registered the offense; 2) the encroacher should be from an Adivasi area;

8. Section 4 of the IFA requires that the government issue a proclamation stating its intent to declare an area a reserved forest. After Campaign for Survival and Dignity 2003).

3) maximum land to be regularised is 8 acres, including other holdings; 4) half of the regularised land must be under agro-forestry. Fine receipts (or an offense noted in the crime register), presentation of documentary evidence of pre-1980 cultivation by organisations, or documentary evidence of benefits received from the Agriculture Department would be the only types of proof accepted.

This GR also clarified that due to the provisions of the Forest Conservation Act 1980, no future cultivations would be authorised and further encroachments would be evicted. This GR also maintained that trees planted before 1980 will belong to government, whereas trees planted by the farmer after 1980 would remain the property of the farmer himself.

7th August 1994

1. Circular issued by the Chief Conservator of Forests (Wildlife), Gujarat state to ban plantations on disputed lands to be regularised. This circular orders the removal of new plantations on such land and guarantees that no new plantations would take place.
2. Circular issued by the Chief Conservator of Forests (Wildlife), Gujarat state. Good quality plantations on 'encroached' lands should be allowed to stand in an attempt to protect the state investment, and bona fide affected cultivators should be given other lands.
3. Circular issued by the Chief Conservator of Forests (Wildlife), Gujarat state. In all cases recommended to government of India for regularisation of land, no fine should be levied from the occupiers but only compensation equal to land revenue would be collected.

16th November 1994

This circular announced that a proposal was sent to the GOI to delete 10,900.47 ha of forest land from the Forest Department records to accommodate regularisation of the pre-1967 cultivation claims. The proposal was granted and that land would now be considered revenue land.

11th August 1997

The first GR regarding regularisation referred to Adivasi areas. This GR now discusses regularisation of cultivations in the eastern forest belt.

3rd August 2000

A memorandum of the Government of Gujarat announced the decision to regularise cultivations before 25th October 1980, per resolution dated October 1992. The Government of India approved the proposal in principal as of 17th October 1994. This memo officially announces that 21,082.33 ha of forest land will be regularised in the name of 34,441 Adivasi farmers per official survey.

9th March 2001

The state memorandum dated 3rd August 2000 claimed to have regularised 21,082.33 ha of forest land to 34,441 eligible encroachers. In 2001, the Gujarat government formed a committee solely of forest department employees and MoEF officials to monitor the process of land distribution.

MoEF Circular: 3rd May 2002

However, by this point, the MoEF released its circular dated 3rd May 2002 regarding the eviction of illegal encroachment of forest lands in various States/ UTs in a time bound manner. This made reference of Supreme Court order of 23rd November 2001 in IA 703 in WP No 202/95, which restrains the central government from regularisation of encroachments. Since this time, confusion and chaos has dominated the state's forest land debate.

MoEF Circular: 21st December 2004

Traditional rights of Adivasis on forest lands, discontinuance of eviction Adivasis thereof. No Adivasis should be evicted until survey is done (ineligible encroachers can be evicted, however)

12th May 2005

A Gujarat Government Resolution championing the traditional rights of Adivasis of forest lands and instructing the discontinuance of eviction. The Resolution clearly states that the 1) Cut off date for regularisation of cultivations is 1980 because of FCA, 2) That only forest dwellers are subject to regularisation of land; 3) applicants must have maintained continuous possession since before 1980; and 5) recognised that an applicant may only be declared ineligible only after survey is done.

A few examples of the kind of problems faced by these settlements are instructive. In the villages of Nandod (Rajpipla) and Sagbara, many Adivasis have revenue receipts dating to the 1960s and 1970s for taxes paid while cultivating revenue wasteland; these cultivations were known as *farati* (rotating). Despite these records, the FSO often recorded far less area than what was actually cultivated. The people continue to cultivate these lands, but these rights were not regularised and no official title was issued. As per the 1992 GR to regularise lands, in 2002 many were finally given deeds for small fractions of the lands they had cultivated.

There are cases where the Forest Department has claimed control over lands that were never officially transferred to them from the Revenue Department. For instance, in the village of Gadi of Dediapada, a villager who had been cultivating wasteland for 30 years lost his land to the Forest Department. In these kinds of villages, fines and taxes have often been extracted from the people by both the Forest Department and the Revenue Department. In some areas, section 20 notifications[9] have never been issued, yet the Forest Department claims the land as its own (Campaign for Survival and Dignity 2003).

Forest land accounts for about 20% of the total land cultivated in the Panchmahals and Dahod, and the Naiks in that area have been cultivating plots on this land for as long as they can remember. In 2006, the FD began evicting cultivators. In many cases people were systematically evicted from forest cultivations, only to have the local sarpanch

9. Section 20 of the IFA 1927 empowers the government to issue a final notification to constitute a reserved forest. Only those areas for which section 20 notifications have been issued are actually reserved forests, though in practice the Forest Departments of all States treat even proposed reserved forests as if they have already been notified. A section 20 notification can only be issued after the completion of the rights settlement process.

subsequently co-opt that land. People do not have title deeds for those lands, and the receipts for the fines they have paid consistently under-report the area under cultivation (where they have fine receipts for land at all). However, the people of the village built up resistance to the FD by filling up trenches dug by the Forest Department and managed to retain their land.

Avinash (2005) has identified the historical barriers to resolving the forest land rights issue in Gujarat. The Government of Gujarat (GoG) has selectively implemented Central policies and legislations. For example, the GoG does not differentiate between 'encroachers', who are cultivating notified forest land without documentation, and 'disputed claimants' who are cultivating lands in which no survey and settlement was ever done. In fact, the central order to settle disputed claims has been omitted in the Gujarat government order on the matter.

All regularisation orders issued by the Gujarat government, like those in other States, require that cultivators prove they were cultivating the concerned land prior to a specified cut-off date. Up until now, fine receipts for fines paid to the Forest Department were the main form of proof that the government accepted for this purpose. But often forest cultivators were fined for acts other than cultivation, such as trespassing, and the resulting receipts did not officially validate the claim to the land. Other cultivators did not preserve their fine receipts. Many were never issued fine receipts, and in the wake of the regularisation orders, the FD has deliberately discontinued issuing fine receipts for cultivation. Moreover, even those with valid fine receipts for cultivation before 1980 were sometimes misled and told that they had passed the time limit to have their land regularised. Those with deeds often actually possessed more land than what was recorded on paper. The name on the title deed is also sometimes different than the person who is actually cultivating the land. Sometimes title deeds for the same plot of land would be issued in the name of two different cultivators. Deeds do not record the actual survey number being cultivated, and hence there are often disputes between the FD and the cultivator regarding the land cultivated. Finally, common grasing land is also often taken over by the FD.

In reality only a minor fraction of forest cultivators have ever benefited from the repeated state promises to regularise cultivation on forest land. It is widely recognised that the political will to execute the government orders has simply been absent. The 1972 Gujarat Government Resolution provided for regularisation of lands cultivated from prior to 1967. According to the Gujarat Forest Department records, only 1,713 hectares of forest land were regularised as a result of this 1972 GR (Xavier 2007). The total area of land recognised as encroachment eligible for regularisation (see Table 16) is only 6.7% of the cumulative area placed under plantations by the FD from 1997-2002 (3.16 lakh hectares) (Xavier 2007). These official figures are gross underestimates of the actual area of forest land that should be regularised, and even what little is accepted by the FD has not yet been fully regularised. The claims filed by cultivators with District Collectors, the Chief Secretary or the DFO and the Gujarat Governor after 2003 alone show a much larger area of forest land under cultivation. As per these forms, at least 50,443 acres of land are being cultivated by forest cultivators (see Table 17)[10]. An estimated total of 1.71 lakh ha have been transferred from the Forest Department to the Revenue Department for cultivation since 1961 (Lobo and Kumar 2007).

10. For example, Dahod, Valsad and Vadodara are not represented at all. This represents the list of claims filed by those in contact with the NGO Rajpipla Social Service Society, on behalf of Adivasi Mahasabha. The total number of claims is much higher.

Table 16: Land to be Regularised in the name of 'Encroachers', per Annexure of Gujarat State Memorandum dated 3rd August 2000

No.	*District*	*Number of encroachers*	*Area (ha)*
1	Banaskantha	181	141.54
2	Sabarkantha	1311	919.84
3	Nadiad	141	65.44
4	Panchmahal	5032	4674.91
5	Dahod	2577	2099.2
6	Vadodara	5732	4434.84
7	Narmada	2291	26.59.80
8	Bharuch	709	871.79
9.	Surat	1312	1543.84
10	Dangs	141	98.5
11	Navsari	4342	1075.69
12	Valsad	10672	2496.94
	TOTAL	34441	21082.33

(Government of Gujarat 2000)

Table 17: Survey of Forest Claims Filed after 2002

Village	*No. of Talukas*	*No. of Villages*	*No. of Cultivators*	*No. of Affected People*	*Amount of Land Under Cultivation (acres)*
Banaskantha	2	85	1669	-	1971
Bharuch	2	-no data-	901	4505	-
Dangs	1	74	1009	6318	6018
Narmada	4	252	6610	38907	32253
Navsari	1	5	130	-	278
Panchmahal	8	55	785	-	3925
Surat	4	75	1314	6595	5988
Total	22	546	12418	56325	50433

Though Adivasi claims to land rights have yet to be settled, forest lands have meanwhile been denotified for the purpose of infrastructure and other projects. After 1981, a total of 35,946 ha of forest land have been transferred for development projects (Lobo and Kumar 2007)[11]. About 18,601 ha of forest land in districts with high Adivasi populations has been denotified for purposes other than cultivation (see Table 18).

Table 18: Decade-wise Forest Land Transferred to Development Projects in Districts with Adivasi Concentration (Area in Hectares)

Circle	*1981-90*	*1991-2000*	*2001-04*	*Total*
Bharuch	21.17	536.36	797.12	1354.65
Surat	6330.06	369.91	120.41	6820.38
Vadodara	157.01	586.44	196.63	940.08
Valsad	1955.75	7523.77	7.23	9486.75
	8463.99	9016.48	1121.39	18601.86

(Taken from: Lobo and Kumar 2007)

Much of the awareness of forest law among Adivasis has been a result of active external support in their fight for forest rights. Much of what is in the public sphere about the forest issue in Gujarat has come out of a practical *need* to know on the part of Adivasis and the various institutions and individuals working with Adivasis. Various people's struggles have shaped our understanding of the forest land issue, and thus we will take a closer look at some of the contemporary organised struggles for forest land in the context of what they achieved and what they taught us. The stories represent the multitude of strategies that may be used in the struggle for forest rights. The unity and solidarity fostered by the forest struggle is unrivalled by any other issue in the experience of the Adivasis of Gujarat. This indicates the importance of forests and forest resources for the people of the Eastern belt.

---

11. As these data regard forest land transferred after 1981, the bulk of the forest land lost to the Ukai and Sardar Sarovar dams is not stated here.

Disha and Ekalavya Sangathan

The non-violent movement for land rights in the Eastern Adivasi belt carried on by Disha and Ekalavya Sangathan played a formative role in making the rights of Adivasis a politically recognised issue at the state level. Jani (2002) argues that the movement led by Ekalavya had a greater impact on Adivasi land rights than did all of the Gandhian satyagrahas, the *boodhan* movement, and the distribution of surplus agricultural land combined. Some 65,950 Adivasis were rendered eligible to take legal possession of 50,961 hectares.

According to a survey done by Disha, 42% of Adivasi cultivators rely solely on forest land cultivation to meet their needs. A sample survey of 461 Adivasis from across the northern part of the indigenous belt of the State showed that they paid an average of Rest 536 in fines, while cultivators in Baria paid as much as Rs. 760 per head (see Table 19).

Table 19: Reliance on Forest Land and Fines Paid

Taluka	*Cultivators of forest land*	*Farmers without any Revenue land*	*Cultivation of land (in Acres)*	*Fine paid (in Rs.)*
Dahod	65	19	283.83	32100.98
Jalod	12	3	24.39	6954.11
Lunawada	68	29	259.84	19849.31
Santrampur	131	112	357.64	55388.21
Shehra	11	1	45.80	6179.02
Godhra	13	1	39.15	6748.21
Baria	84	7	350.62	63868.78
Limkheda	77	26	336.04	56076.94
Total	461	198	1652.31	247166.16

Mobilisation of the masses and numerous agitations since 1986 finally forced the state Government to acknowledge the 1990 Central circulars regarding the recognition of forest land rights. The movement ensured that 1) as per the Central Government's order, the state would set up a committee to supervise recognition of rights over lands cultivated up to October 1980 in favour of Adivasis; 2) occupants of disputed lands would be allowed to remain in possession of their lands until the procedure of regularisation is complete; 3) afforestation programmes taken up on post-1980 cultivated land will give priority to Adivasis for employment, and the profits of such programs should go to the Adivasis.

The 1992 Government Resolution that provided for these matters was not, however, implemented. In 1994, Ekalavya threatened another mass demonstration, which prompted the state government to recommend to the central government that 39,750 ha of forest land be regularised in the name of the rightful Adivasi cultivators. Jani reports that titles for land cultivated before 1967 (as per the 1972 GR) were completely distributed after a decade of mobilisation and agitation, but distribution of title for lands cultivated up to 1980 (as per the 1992 GR) still continues.

Implementation of forest rights through the judiciary: ARCH Vahini

The NGO ARCH intervened in 1989 by filing a case saying that the FD was impinging on the Adivasi farmers' right to live by imposing fines (of up to Rs. 500) on them for cultivating forest land without documentary proof of possession. Those who could not pay were served notices for eviction. According to the Indian Forest Act, 1927, the maximum fine that can be levied is Rs. 50. ARCH cited Article 254 of the constitution, which states that a Central legislation will take primacy over a state legislation if any conflict between the two exists. ARCH won the case, and the practice of exorbitant fee extraction was halted.

The Central Pulp Mill (based in Songadh) is responsible for mass bamboo extraction in the southern forest belt. From 1960–2000, this paper mill was given a lease by the Government of Gujarat to extract bamboo from the forest. The lease included an area that later became part of the Shoolpaneshwar Wildlife Sanctuary. The declaration of the sanctuary resulted in restrictions on the rights of Adivasi residents, but the paper mill continued bamboo extraction. The Gujarat High Court granted permission for the continued exploitation of the bamboo from the sanctuary despite the provisions of the Wild Life (Protection) Act and Supreme Court orders in the *Godavaraman* case[12]. It was not until the Supreme Court's Central Empowered Committee, set up in Godavarman, intervened in the matter that the bamboo extraction was halted. The Committee however never addressed the legality of the lease itself, nor did it recommend the filing of contempt of court charges against the erring Government of Gujarat (Parekh 2004).

In 2005, ARCH filed a public interest litigation against the state of Gujarat on behalf of 2,000 Adivasi families who were cultivating 3,000 hectares of 'forest land' in Sagbara block of Narmada district (see Box: 2 Gross State Negligence And Alienation of Forest Land). Though these were really disputed lands where no survey had taken place, the Adivasis' plots were treated as encroachments. This was clearly in violation of the 1972 GR to regularise cultivations that had begun prior to 1967, and the 1992 GR to regularise cultivations that had begun prior to 1980. A stay order was issued by the court. Currently the claims are being processed under the Forest Rights Act, 2006.

Box 2

Gross State Negligence And Alienation of Forestland

Bhils of Sagbara had been cultivating lands granted by the local Vasava Chieftain for generations. Upon the emergence of Bombay state, the Vasava Chieftain became the superior land holder of the Sagbara Estate while individual Adivasis were recognised as inferior land holders. The Sagbara estate was then dismantled in 1962 by the Sagbara and Mehwasi Estates (Proprietary Rights Abolition) Regulation, 1962, and the Adivasis

---

12. *T.N. Godavarman Thirumalpad and Ors. vs. Union of India and Ors.*, WP 202/95.

became the deemed occupants. Unfortunately, land was regularised in the names of Adivasi families only in easily accessible areas and the process was incomplete in the interior hilly regions. Because of the incomplete survey, land was registered into the state records as culturable wasteland even where the Adivasi citizenry possess the land deeds they received from the Chieftain in exchange for a fee. The people continued to cultivate these lands as occupants and paid annual revenue to the state.

Meanwhile by 1975, the Government of Gujarat declared all of Sagbara taluka's wastelands as Reserve Forest. Section 4 was declared under the Indian Forest Act 1927, yet entry of the notification showed up in the village records in 1990. In this way the Revenue Department and the Forest Department both exerted their command over the same region for a decade-and-a-half. The Forest Settlement Officer (FSO) himself found that 2000 individuals were tilling 3000 hectares of land through his survey of the 12,000 hectare region. The FSO denied his legal obligation to strike down the notification on cultivated lands, and instead devised an arbitrary system to determine legitimate claims. He decided that only 160 cultivators, farming 165 hectares of land, whose names were registered in the village revenue records before 1960, had legal title to the land. The FSO decided that 520 cultivators tilling 900 ha of land would be given a right to cultivate without legal ownership – through a lease-type arrangement with the forest department. The rest of the 1300 cultivators tilling 2000 ha of land were recommended for eviction. Thus ARCH took the case to court.

National solidarity with the forest struggle: Adivasi Mahasabha

Adivasi Mahasabha (AMS), a coalition of people's organisations committed to Adivasi issues in Gujarat state, was formed in 2002 in response to the threat of forest evictions, which had intensified after the 3rd May 2002 order of the Inspector General of Forests[13]. This group has sustained a string of people's protests that eventually helped force the passage of the Scheduled Tribes and Other Traditional Forest Dwellers (Recognition of Forest Rights) Act, 2006, in Parliament. AMS was linked to the national forest rights movement under the banner of the Campaign for Survival and Dignity. Never has a people's movement for forest rights in Gujarat been so closely linked with a concerted national effort to agitate for legal change at the Central level.

After the 2002 order, the FD became bolder in their eviction attempts; according to the Ministry of Environment and Forests, as on 31st March 2004, 14,416.86 hectares of 'encroachments' had been evicted after the IGF order. In the Dangs, twenty-two farmers who had filed claims for regularising their pre-1980 forest cultivations were arrested on bogus charges in the summer of 2004. After the monsoon of 2004, 39 farming families had their standing crops destroyed by the Forest Department. An estimated Rs. 4.69 lakhs of crops were destroyed and police complaints were lodged. In 2004, there were four documented cases of people who were beaten simply for cultivating forest land. Such cases were documented by the AMS network throughout the eastern tribal belt. Besides documentation of atrocities, AMS made numerous representations to officials within the state machinery from the block up to the state level.

Connecting state and national level coalition strengthened the movement in several ways. First, the ground realities and lessons learned were constantly being conveyed not only within the state among member organisations, but also to the national level. This allowed for creating strategies at multiple levels – from local to national. Because the people have been plagued from the start with a lack of transparency, this constant exchange of knowledge became critical to

13. This order required all State governments to remove all 'encroachers' before 30th September 2002. It resulted in massive and brutal evictions across India.

efficient and decisive action. The geographic spread of member organisations and their communities allowed for consistent local demonstrations as well as stronger pressure on the state government.

The national coalition lobbied parliament and called national mobilisations and demonstrations. Eventually, a landmark (though imperfect) act recognising the traditional forest rights of Adivasis was passed. Currently AMS is taking the lead in Gujarat in ensuring that the Scheduled Tribes and Other Traditional Forest Dwellers (Recognition of Forest Rights) Act, 2006 is implemented in letter and spirit. The group continues to consolidate the efforts of a multitude of people's organisations to fight for forest rights.

A detailed look at the Dangs

Forest resources and forest cultivation are inextricable for the existence of the Dangis. The FD is practically the only large landlord – hardly any land alienation has happened in the favour of non-Adivasis in this district, and thus the state is directly responsible for alienation of ancestral lands. The Dangis tended to have oral leases with erstwhile rulers in the pre-Independence era. These have not been respected by the Government of India or the FD. In the context of the 1992 GR to regularise pre-1980 cultivations, the Forest Department claims to have received applications from 404 forest cultivators covering 599.7 hectares of forest land in the Dangs. Of those 404 applications, a mere 43 persons (10%) were granted land because only these 43 persons possessed fine receipts. Whereas the Ministry of Environment and Forests allowed for other types of proof of cultivation, such as affidavits and evidence from the former rulers of Dangs, the Government of Gujarat did not. The Gujarat High Court unconstitutionally ruled against the people in a civil application (1998) to the court challenging this.

In the 1960s, 79,913 acres of land was classified as farmland based on a government survey; this was 45% of the total area of the district. The area of farmland declined to less than one-third of this figure by the 1990s. Whereas the Forest Department claims that the land was voluntarily surrendered to the Department, nothing about the history or the spirit of the Dangi people lends credibility to this claim. Unofficial reports suggest that, for instance, 726 Bhil farmers spread over 18 villages continue to cultivate 4,493 acres of 'forest' land (Rajiv Shah, in Engineer 2002). A writ petition filed in the Gujarat High Court referred to 1,892 hectares cultivated by 228 Adivasis spread over 20 villages (Engineer 2002).

The official numbers highly under-report the actual number of claims. As of 2004, a total of 3,050 claims for the regularisation of forest land rights had been filed in the Dangs. When the DFO of Dangs was asked to address these claims by the District Collector, he responded only to 25% – and rejected all of these. Even those with fine receipts were rejected based on circular logic: all pre-1980 claims had already been regularised, thus any new claims would not be entertained. Those without fine receipts were rejected for not having legitimate proof.

One key element in the history of forest rights in the Dangs is the role played by forest labour cooperatives. In the spirit of *Sarvodaya*, Gandhian activists have a history of working in the forested interiors of Gujarat. With the desire to provide an alternative to communist agitations against landlords, moneylenders and forest contractors, they formed the first forest labour cooperative in Bombay state in 1947 (Joshi 1997). Jugatram Dave, a Gandhian, followed suit in Surat in 1948. These cooperatives improved working conditions reasonably and came to provide a political base for Gandhian activists in the state. Similar cooperatives in the Dangs were important to help the Dangis survive on the meagre land holdings they had and reduced migration out of the area. In 1962, after the Dangs became part of Gujarat State, the state government moved to liquidate all the Maharashtrian forest labour cooperatives. Cooperatives were again formed in 1967; in the interim period, the Forest

Department and contractors carried out all tree cutting. The leaders of the forest cooperatives held tremendous power since they controlled who would have access to forestry employment; their local clout got them elected to the district panchayat, and thereby increased their political power by giving them discretion over government funds. These powers and funds were abused, and corruption saw to it that the Dangi Adivasis hardly reaped any benefit from the booming timber economy that they fed. In 1986, the MoEF at the central level declared a ban on all cutting of trees in reserved forests; the forest labour cooperatives thus lost their base. Conservation activities have not provided sufficient substitute labour, and thus the communities that used to depend on these cooperatives are now being forced to migrate (Joshi 1997).

The Dangs have witnessed strong people's movements for land rights. *Adivasi Bhoomiheen Kisan Hakk Saurakshan Samiti* (Adivasi Farmland Rights Protection Committee), started in 1989, is a good example of the organised side of such struggles. Irfan Engineer from Bombay and Virsingh Vishram (an Adivasi) from Surat, two leftist activists, initiated the formation of this committee, which was created in response to forest guards' confiscation of wood under the pretext that it had been cut from the reserved forest. Women protested these illegal confiscations, and the movement that resulted gained support across the various Adivasi communities – Bhils, Konkanas, and Varlis. The committee had eleven main demands: 1) resettlement of the 110 villages that had been ousted from the reserved forest in their original locations; 2) a new survey of cultivated lands; 3) grant of ownership of trees to the occupier of the land; 4) rights to forest produce; 5) a living wage for labour; 6) just market price for produce; 7) an end to Forest Department harassment and punitive measures for violators; 8) annual employment provision to end migration; 9) forest and agro-industry development in Dangs; 10) basic infrastructure development; 11) free education to all Dangis at Ahwa.

In 1991, members of the *Samiti* performed an even bolder action when they cleared a section of the reserved forest and demanded that their right to that land – which was a part of their old village – be recognised. In the subsequent clash, though the police had guns, the Dangis were armed with bows and arrows and slingshots. State repression followed shortly. In 1990-91, several local activists and those involved with the Committee's work were beaten, molested, harassed, and one - Taraben Pawar - was shot dead in an encounter with the Forest Department. Irfan and Virsingh were arrested and jailed under the National Security Act. These events generated a good amount of negative publicity outside of the Dangs. Irfan and Virsingh were eventually released unconditionally in 1990 and the NSA charges dropped (Joshi 1997).

Today, Dangis tend mostly to be self-cultivators. They are now confronted with land scarcity, which is aggravated by the state's emphasis on commercial development of the forest (Engineer 2002). As changes in land ownership are not recorded on paper, the holdings are more meagre than what official records depict. The Department continues to encroach on the lands of the people; for instance, in one case the Department conducted plantation work on 20 acres of private land. Such land grabbing only pushes tillers further to cultivate more forest land. The small size of land holdings is particularly problematic as the fertility of the Dangi highland soil is already low, and the people do not have the money to invest in improvements. It is virtually unknown for the land to ever produce a surplus crop that can be sold in the market. Roughly 50% of the farmers are unable to produce the food grains they require for a full year and run out before the next season begins. This forces half of the population to migrate to the plains for harvesting sugar cane. Other sources of employment include Central Pulp Mills (Songadh, Surat district) and harvesting of minor forest produce, such as *tendu* leaves for bidis (Engineer 2002).

Contemporary schemes under the Adivasi Sub-plan in

the Dangs benefit only the few elites who can provide the cash inputs necessary to maintain infrastructure such as wells and the like (Trivedi 1980). The state is more concerned with improving revenue from the forest than it is with the welfare of the people. The Forest Department and others benefit from the miserable economic conditions of the Dangi Adivasis, who are treated as a reserve of cheap, desperate labour. The Central Paper Mills paid extremely low wages to Dangi Adivasis (Rs 120 per tonne of bamboo cut). Similar conditions apply in cane harvesting and various other commercial agricultural operations (Engineer 2002).

2.4 Land Acquisition for Development

State-led land acquisition in the name of development is a contemporary problem that is devastating the Adivasi community. In Gujarat, state prioritisation of so-called infrastructure and economic development has repeatedly trumped the welfare of Adivasis.. Since Independence, over 31.22 lakh hectares of land have been acquired by the Government of Gujarat under the Land Acquisition Act, based on the principle of eminent domain. Land acquisition has several direct effects on Adivasi communities, primarily from displacement of people whose land has been acquired. Acquisition, through displacement, alienates communities from their traditional resource base, while simultaneously breaking down traditional kin networks that are the basis of Adivasi life and economy. Lack of prior exposure to the external world renders most Adivasis unable to adjust to mainstream life. Those who are on the borders of these acquired lands are impacted by the environmental and ecological changes resulting from these so-called development projects. This type of infrastructure provides practically no benefits to Adivasi areas. Thus, while infrastructure for agriculture is lacking – e.g. agriculture is mostly rain fed, and there is no lift irrigation in many areas – the area booms with infrastructure for industry. The true human and environmental cost is thus externalised by

Table 20: Category-wise and Decade-wise Land Acquisition in Gujarat 1947-2004 (in Hectares)

Categories	*1947-1960*	*% share*	*1961-1980*	*% share*	*1981-1990*	*% share*	*1991-2004*	*% share*	*Grand total*	*% share*
Water Resources	32,260.8	13.9	674,050.2	56.6	689,957.5	66.9	522,123.5	78.2	1,918,392.0	61.4
Industries	2,891.2	1.2	40,741.0	3.4	87,181.2	8.5	49,415.3	7.4	180,228.6	5.8
Mines	24.3	0.0	29.9	0.0	2,089.6	0.2	4,918.8	0.7	7,062.6	0.2
Non-Hydel	178.6	0.1	5,727.7	0.5	8,507.0	0.8	1,874.0	0.3	16,287.3	0.5
Defence and Security	59.7	0.0	860.8	0.1	4,981.0	0.5	889.6	0.1	6,791.2	0.2
Environment Protection	16.5	0.0	1,542.7	0.1	289.0	0.0	0.0	0.0	1,848.1	0.1
Transport and Communication	168,626.9	72.6	309,046.0	25.9	175,048.6	17.0	67,081.0	10.0	719,802.5	23.1
Human Resources	9,634.2	4.1	51,045.4	4.3	9,371.8	0.9	374.1	0.1	70,425.4	2.3
Farm and Fisheries	1,079.9	0.5	1,837.0	0.2	826.3	0.1	2.9	0.0	3,746.0	0.1
Urban Development	13,605.2	5.9	75,257.9	6.3	32,137.1	3.1	15,917.8	2.4	136,917.9	4.4
Refugee Resettlement	7.8	0.0	67.3	0.0	0.0	0.0	794.2	0.1	869.3	0.0
Social welfare	1,023.1	0.4	23,602.5	2.0	5,444.0	0.5	317.5	0.0	30,387.0	1.0
Tourism	131.0	0.1	283.3	0.0	99.2	0.0	112.0	0.0	625.4	0.0
Government Offices	771.8	0.3	2,953.5	0.2	14,626.0	1.4	3,361.1	0.5	21,712.4	0.7
Unknown	2,020.2	0.9	4,860.2	0.4	285.8	0.0	350.9	0.1	7,517.1	0.2
Total	232,331.1	100.0	1,191,905.2	100.0	1,030,844.1	100.0	667,532.5	100.0	3,122,612.9	100.0

Lobo and Kumar, 2006

industries and shifted onto disempowered Adivasi communities.

Infrastructure and industry have driven land acquisition in Gujarat in a way that ensures private profit while eroding common property rights over land, forests, and water – and thus infringing on the Adivasis' right to life. Lobo and Kumar (2007) have studied all notifications pertaining to land acquisition in Gujarat and provide data on the details of these acquisitions. Water resources (61.4%), transport and communication (23.1%) and industries (5.8%) account for the vast majority of land acquired (see Figure 5).

A sample survey designed to look at the community break-down of the displaced revealed that members of scheduled tribes bear the brunt of land acquisition for government projects. STs form 42% of the project affected population but 76% of those displaced (see Table 20). Much of this displacement directly results from the construction of dams.

Figure 5: Land Acquired for Selected Large and Medium Dams (1947-2004)

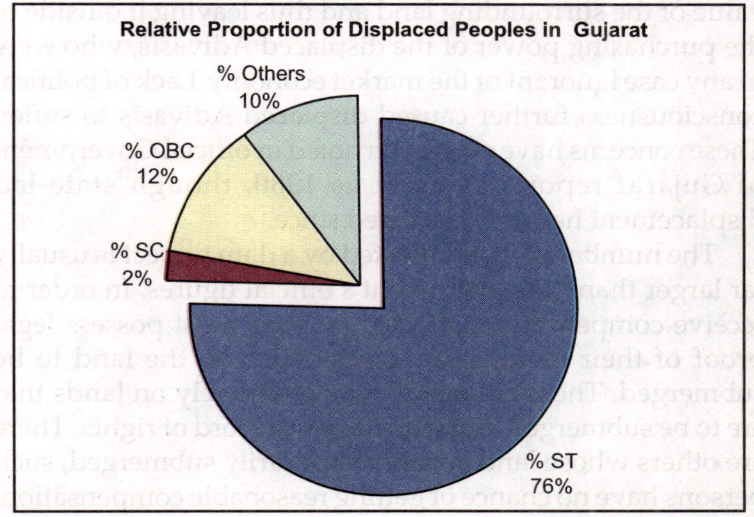

Lobo and Kumar 2007

Water

The operative development paradigm is one in which all major irrigation projects strip Adivasis of their lands and livelihood, while benefiting non-Adivasis downstream. The Ukai, Sardar Sarovar, and Kadana dams are some of the major dams in Gujarat, all of which displaced Adivasis (see Table 21 for a list of major dams in areas with ST populations in Gujarat, with official estimates of affected peoples). During the initial boom of the big-dam concept, the Land Acquisition Act, 1894 was the only piece of legislation the government abided by, and there was no discussion of land-for-land compensation. Effectively, any displaced people automatically became landless. State infrastructure projects levelled a two-fold punishment against Adivasis because they existed outside of the mainstream cash-economy. Adivasi lands were acquired at depreciated rates because they were in the midst of forests – land that historically held no commercial real estate value. There was thus no 'market' rate to assess the land against. However, the development of a dam would invert the scenario, causing a surge in the market value of the surrounding land and thus leaving it outside of the purchasing power of the displaced Adivasis, who were in any case ignorant of the market economy. Lack of political consciousness further caused displaced Adivasis to suffer. These concerns have even been noted in official Government of Gujarat reports as early as 1980, though state-led displacement has only escalated since.

The number of those affected by a dam project is usually far larger than the government's official figures. In order to receive compensation, affected persons must possess legal proof of their ownership of/residence on the land to be submerged. There are many people who rely on lands that are to be submerged, but who have no record of rights. There are others whose land is only temporarily submerged; such persons have no chance of getting reasonable compensation. A couple cultivating a patch of land at the bank of the Tapi

Table 21: Selected Dams in ST areas

Project Name	*Land Acquired (Ha)*	*Affected Families (includes non ST)*
Sardar Sarovar Project	424919.05	46272
Ukai	215199.4	45253
Kakrapara	2139.94	1195
Mahi Stage 1	60917.81	23450
Mahi Stage 2	3759.19	568
Dharoi	149988.16	20101
Damanganga	49632.05	9823
Karjan	60146.83	9499
Panam	53510.25	3446
Sipu and Mukteshwar	48007.13	4034
Sukhi	23912.37	3359
Kadana	62714.02	5271
Dantiwada	11851.78	4744

Lobo and Kumar, 2006.

river report that the Ukai dam submerged their farmland during the monsoon. They are hence able to harvest a crop only in the summer, when yields are highly unreliable. The Vasavas of this area are traditionally rice-eaters, but the couple can no longer grow their own rice and must purchase from the market. They must work as agricultural labour on the fields of others to survive.

Even the Ministry of Rural Development acknowledges that there is discrepancy between the official statistics and independent reviews on the effects of dams. For example, the Ministry of Rural Development reports that there are no official statistics for the number of people who were displaced by the Ukai dam.

Rehabilitation packages are deeply flawed. For instance, colonies and people affected by the canal network of the Narmada dam are not eligible for the award of the Narmada Water Disputes Tribunal. Six villages in the Kevadia area, comprised of 800 families, were displaced from 1961-1987. Even though the concerned dam site was eventually shifted, these displaced people were not given their lands back. Most of the rehabilitation sites for the Narmada dam are in the command area, which is prone to water logging (Narmada IPT 2004). In 2004, most of the rehabilitation sites were flooded by the monsoon rain and the relocated farmers suffered significant loss of crops (Narmada IPT 2004).

In another example, the Ukai reservoir submerged 27 villages in Sagbara block. This was one of the first times when an organised movement demanded compensation from the state for dam-induced displacement. Rameshbhai Desai, through *Ukai Navnirman Samiti*, negotiated a settlement of up to Rs. 900/acre; this was considered historic. However, there were also many who received no compensation at all, despite losing lands cultivated for generations. In the case of the Ukai dam, the state allotted reservoir land on a yearly lease basis for use during the summer time, when the waters recede. However, this was eventually discontinued due to forest conservation requirements; the government claimed that afforestation was affected by the practice (Patel 2007). Today, about 35% of women affected by the Ukai dam complain that they have not been able to find alternative employment after being displaced (Lobo and Kumar 2007).

Though section 73AA[14] of the Revenue Code in theory protects Adivasis from land alienation, the state regularly exercises its acquisition powers as if it were an agent for private interests seeking to alienate these lands. The majority of land acquired for industrial purpose by the Gujarat Industrial Development Corporation is Adivasi land, which is then in turn leased back to private parties in order to earn hefty profits. The government simply acts as a middleman and an agent for Adivasi exploitation. In Bharuch, this has ironically meant that non-Adivasis were able to sell their land

14. Prohibits land transfer from Adivasis to Adivasis from the date of issuance of this amendment. Land alienation from an Adivasi to another Adivasi that took place between 1960 and 1980 will be upheld.

for Rs. 30,000-40,000 per acre, while Adivasi lands are acquired by the state at Rs. 5,000 per acre (Judge 1999).

Industry

A disproportionately high number of hazardous industries have come up in Bharuch district. Fifteen-thousand acres of land in the district, a tribal majority district, has been diverted for industrial purposes such as chemical industries as well as mining in Jhagadia. These are all water-intensive industries and have had enormous impacts on not just the local communities, but on the entire region. Drinking water has been polluted, and agricultural productivity has declined in neighbouring areas. The Ankleshvar industrial estate reportedly consumes 100 MW of electricity and guzzles over 45 million litres of water from the Ukai canal. In return, the region is rewarded with 40,000 tonnes of hazardous waste, and the waters of river Narmada are polluted with 32 million litres of toxic effluent (IPT 1999). In the monsoon season, the canals carrying effluent-contaminated waters flood over into agricultural land, destroying crops. A similar picture is presented in Nandesari.

The Gujarat Industrial Development Corporation (GIDC) acquired about 1,700 hectares of land for the Jhagadia Industrial Estate in 1997 to house chemical industries. Non-Adivasi Rajputs and Muslims landlords happily contributed the greatest share of the land, selling their properties to the GIDC at over 5.5 times the going rate in the area. Non-Adivasis also sold their lands directly to industries (Pinto, not dated). Approximately 1,338 ha of land were then leased out for mining. Lignite and agate are the main ores that are produced in this mining area. Other mined materials in the area include calcite, ball clay, dolomite, illuminate, limestone, silica sand, and sandstone (Pinto, not dated).

Many Adivasis in the area report that the government refused to recognise their legal rights over lands they cultivated since 1965. Thus people in villages such as Tarsali, Amaljar, and Bhuri, live in fear of total displacement by mining. The range of effects on the local Adivasi population, primarily those residing in the villages of Amod, Maljipura, and Bhimpore, are complex and mostly irreversible. The continual expansion of the Gujarat Mining Development Corporation (GMDC) projects in the area remains a looming threat to the people. In its Environmental Impact Assessment (EIA) report in connection with its application for expansion clearance in 2004, GMDC falsely claimed that no agricultural labourers would be affected by its operations. The report neglected to give any details on the rehabilitation package for displaced communities – who in this case were being displaced for the *second* time by this corporation. The EIA report also omitted mentioning that the water table is so depleted that drinking water must be brought in by tanker, that GMDC is dumping acidic wastewater into nearby *nallahs*, and that the slope of over-burden dumps have not been maintained. By its own assessment, over 40 tons of heavy metal waste is stored on site in a pit with no impervious liner, allowing for the hazardous materials to leach into the soil and ground water (Mazgaonkar 2004). Leases to extract these commodities are granted to private, non-Adivasi parties, thus placing resources of Adivasis in the hands of non-Adivasis. The activities of GMDC, therefore, pose a constant threat to the health, livelihood, and physical existence of the Adivasis of the region. Nor is GMDC the only mining corporation; Gujarat Industries Power Company Limited (GIPCL) acquired some 36 square kilometres of land for lignite mining in Mangrol block of Surat district. This again is an ST majority block. Mining disturbs water bodies, reduces land fertility, creates acid rain due to sulphur releases into the atmosphere, contributes to climate change through carbon dioxide releases, and contaminates the environment with various carcinogens – essentially devastating agriculture in the region and impacting health.

But mining is not the only threat. In Kharvel village of Valsad district, 14 of 37 entries in land transfer records between 1985 and 1997 concerned transfers to factories (pharmaceutical and chemical manufacturing and food processing). In Morai Village, between 1981 and 1992, 35 of 76 land transactions were made for the purpose of establishing paper mills and stone quarries. In Khurelia village, the Department of Irrigation acquired lands at throwaway prices to build a canal. In addition to losing land in such acquisitions, the local residents also must contend with the repercussions of these businesses – like polluted drinking water and hazardous solid waste. The Sarpanch of Kharvel reports that land is acquired through power-of-attorney letters, leaving villagers ignorant of the transactions. The lands are then converted from agricultural to non-agricultural land without permission. In addition, Jani and Ganguly have observed that most land transfers occur within the Adivasi community. This has led to the creation of an Adivasi elite, whose wealth is self-perpetuating (Jani and Ganguly 2000).

Lal (1992) describes Vapi, Valsad and Pardi as a 'cluster of isolated Adivasi villages which is now emerging as the most important industrial region of the Gujarat State'. Vapi industrial estate was established in 1967. Chemical industries and pulp paper mills dominate in the estate. This has led to environmental degradation, particularly of water sources and forest land. The fishing communities of Kolak and Daman villages have been impacted by the decline in the fish population that has taken place as a result of pollution of the Daman-Ganga river. Fruit yields in this area declined by 50%. The industries shrug off the burden of their environmental degradation by dumping waste in land-fills, which leaches toxins into the soil, further reducing productivity (IPT 1999).

Dhodias, Naikas, Halpatis, and Koknas have suffered most from the damage caused by these industries. Communities with less access to land, and those that have been historically worse off (the Halpatis and the Naikas, for example), respond through migration to industrial settings, whereas landed tribes (such as Dhodias) send family members to work in industries but in lesser numbers (Lal

1992). Most industrial workers have 0 to 5 acres of land. By 1992, 37.42% of the residents of this area were industrial workers, whereas only 62% still relied on agriculture for livelihood.

Power generation for urban Gujarat has had major consequences for Adivasis. In addition to the lignite mining mentioned above, Kakarapara Nuclear Power Plant in Surat District has had a manifold impact on the economy and culture of Adivasis. Land was first acquired for the plant itself, disrupting local agriculture. Second, the high levels of radiation emitted from the plant can have effects on local crops and can induce male infertility in some cases.

Danta block is home to the Ambaji base metal project. The GMDC initiated copper mining; lead and zinc deposits are also present. Deposits of limestone attracted the cement industry, specifically Radhakrishna Cement Factory. Danta also has the largest deposits of marble in the state, and is known for high quality white and green marble (Shukla et al 1990).

Cooption of Common Property Resources

Adivasis' lives and economy are heavily based on common property resources, forest and otherwise. Fuel and fodder needs in particular are generally met through common property lands. In modern times, these resources are managed by the revenue department, panchayat department and the forest department. The conversion of lands to non-agricultural use across the board is jeopardising the ability of people to meet many daily requirements. Agricultural land has been diverted recklessly for non-agricultural purposes. The grasing lands, which are the most important element of common property resources, have shrunk over time. With the rising livestock population, the ratio of grasing land to livestock population has declined (Iyengar 2002). Iyengar argues that land reforms, mechanisation of agriculture, and a cultural shift away from self-regulation of common property land have disrupted the balance between private land and common land (Iyengar 2002). Though the total cultivable area of Gujarat state remains steady at about 65%, the productivity of lands varies dramatically. His study of 25 villages found that diversion of agricultural land for non-agricultural purposes has increased across all productivity classes. This has happened despite the fact that the human and cattle populations across the state – and their needs for fuel and fodder – have steadily increased (Iyengar 2002).

The state's emphasis on industrial development directly effects the availability of land for Adivasis. Between 1980 and 1999, the area under non-agricultural use increased by 1,000 hectares (see Table 22). This is in sharp contrast to the amount available to the public as common property over time; between 1970 and 1996, grasing lands decreased by 1,000 hectares (see Figure 6). Common property land in Gujarat overall has decreased by 5% between 1970 and 1996. The public lost about 10,231 square kilometers of common property land. We see this trend amongst all categories of wasteland, but the major loss has happened within the categories classified as barren wasteland and cultivatable wasteland.

Table 22: Land Use Classification Changes Over Time for all of Gujarat

Gujarat-Wide Land Use	*Area in thousands of Hectares* 1980-81	1985-86	1990-91	1995-96	1998-99
Forest land	19655	18777	18847	18628	18647
Non-Agricultural Land	25034	26747	26092	26008	26034
Cultivatable Wasteland	10670	10891	11221	11371	11408
Grazing land	8483	8463	8457	8484	8489

Source: Directorate of Agriculture, Gujarat State. (Compiled by Janpath)

Figure 6: Common Property Land Resources in Gujarat in 1970 and 1996

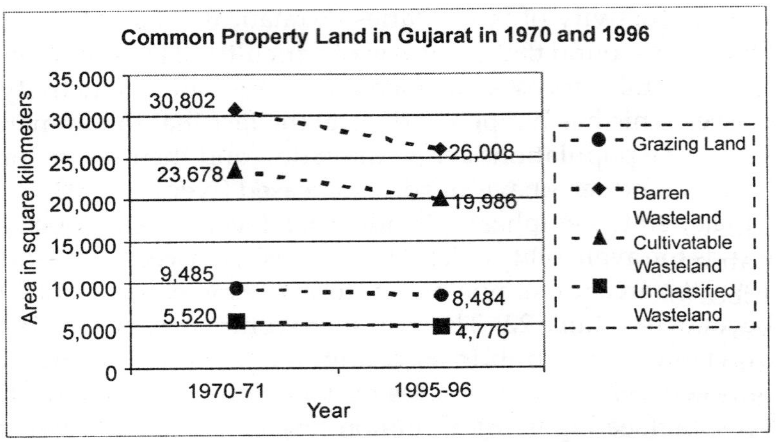

Gujarat Ecology Commission Website (www. gec.gov.in)

Wastelands have also been re-distributed to individual and cooperative farmers for cultivation. Private ownership of land, including by Adivasis themselves, has thus put a significant dent in common property resources. Statistics from the Directorate of Land Reforms regarding the state-wise distribution of wasteland to Adivasis report that Gujarat has distributed 13.81 lakh acres of land. However, the collectors of districts with significant ST populations hardly possess any records to back up this figure.

Despite the demonstrated harmful effects of diminishing common property resources, the state continues to facilitate access to public lands for corporate profit. A 2005 Government Resolution announced that the Gujarat Government plans to give over thousands of acres of land to corporations for cultivation. In the name of 'modern agriculture', Gujarat is handing over wastelands at throwaway rates with lease conditions clearly biased towards the corporate lessee (G R dated 17th May 2005). Thousands of people rely on such wastelands, including Adivasis, Dalits, Maldharis, and others.

3

Gender and Land

Most Adivasi communities in Gujarat are traditionally patriarchal[15], patrilocal[16], and patrilineal[17]. The majority of tribes follow similar inheritance patterns regarding land, with varying rigidity. There is a clear sense of private property and land as private property in the historical memory of the current living generations. Ownership of land will generally be held in the name of the eldest male of a joint-family until his death, upon which land passes on in equal parts to his children (most often sons). Until the time of death, *de facto* partitions will exist, but such partitions usually become part of the official government record only after the patriarch's death. Generally ancestral property and self-acquired property will be divided up equally among the heirs. Because ownership is patrilineal in most Adivasi societies of Gujarat, the right of a woman to hold land is considered nominal and thus women possess limited property rights with respect to land. The problem of fragmentation of holdings is used as justification for withholding land from daughters. Because of the patrilineal system, daughters habitually marry outside of the village and would then be responsible for 'losing' land to another lineage and thus dividing up the space for cultivation. This is particularly a concern when the family survives on agriculture alone, but the daughter marries into

15. Quality of being dominated by men.
16. System of residing with or near the male line of the family; living with one's father or husband's father.
17. Quality of being inherited through the male line; belonging to the father's lineage.

a family that relies on cash income from a job. Thus daughters tend to inherit land only when they continue to live in their native village after marriage. Widows might be given land on a usufruct basis if they have children, remain unmarried and live with their in-laws; once the children come of age, land will be passed on to them. In some communities, it is common for a daughter to inherit from her parents if her marital home is near her native place, and if the family perceives that there is enough land to meet the needs of sons. In the case of multiple wives, property is generally first divided amongst the wives equally and then the children of each wife are given rights to their mother's share.

In a sample survey conducted among the total population of Gujarat, only 11.81% of land owners were women (WGWLO, 2004). As Shilpa Vasavda reports, the Adivasi *Panch* often questions an heirless widow's land rights by suggesting that she has no need for land. A woman's right over land is thus made usufruct in nature, and not alienable. There is irony in the fact that this is precisely the line of logic that non-Adivasis have put forth in order to justify the impermanent land tenancy of Adivasis. Polygynous men, supported by community leaders and the state administration, often deny land titles to one wife (Vasavda 2006). While overall social and legal structures are designed to limit the control women have over land, the many cases of '*ghar jamais*' in Adivasi Gujarat should also be noted. Anecdotal evidence suggest that Adivasi fathers often recruited husbands for daughters in newly settled areas. This is the case of Mozda village, where some of the female elders alive today are the daughters of the first settlers of these areas. As such, the original settlers of these lands passed on their claimed plots to their daughters as well as sons. There are also many cases of brides who came from adjacent, newly settled forested areas who then inherited land in their native village among Bhil communities.

Among Adivasis, there is no cultural practice of the giving of dowry by a girl's family to a boy's – rather, bride price prevails amongst Gujarat Adivasis. For that reason, there is no social mechanism through which a daughter receives property. Today women feel the disadvantage of not owning land, and various NGOs and movements are pushing for women's land rights to be institutionalised. Women are not in a position to apply for loans on the basis of their land when the land is not in their name. With increased male migration, women are left to tend the fields and manage agriculture. The introduction of the cash economy promotes gender inequity since the work that women traditionally do on the farm is less valued and glamorous than the work to be found outside. Because of the general practice of hypergamy[18] even amongst the Adivasis, some Adivasi families are worried about giving land to daughters, who will in any case have a better economic position than their sons.

While women have participated in various Adivasi land rights struggles in Gujarat, the rights of women have not been independently and systematically asserted in such struggles. Various feminist organisations that have been fighting for the empowerment of women have recognised the importance of land rights, and formed a network called the Working Group on Women and Land Ownership (WGWLO) in order to mainstream the issue of land ownership among women's organisations. WGWLO has provided support to NGOs and CBOs working on the distribution of land between the genders. To our knowledge, however, there is no group that is devoted exclusively to land rights among Adivasi women. Women's organisations are so stretched meeting the demands of their agendas that documentation regarding the successes and failures of Adivasi women's land rights struggles is limited. The vast reach of NGOs in Gujarat has sensitised women to their rights and enabled women to become active on issues related to their needs. As a result, there is considerable potential for women associated with NGOs to strengthen the Adivasi land

18. Marrying above one's class.

rights movements. The initial stages of such a pairing are visible through the forest rights movement.

The NGO Anandi (Area Networking and Development Initiatives) is an excellent example of how NGO support has been used to train local women Adivasi activists to take on issues related to land rights. *Devgadh Mahila Sangathan* is a women's union supported by Anandi. In the *Sangathan's* working area, a hamlet of 7 brothers in Sagtala village (Dahod) lost their farmland in 1977 because of a small dam built to create a tank for irrigation. The hamlet belongs to the Naik tribe. The *Sarpanch* approached them regarding acquisition of their land, but never presented any formal notice. They insisted on land-for-land compensation. Eventually, some 16 acres of forest land in the nearby village of Mandav village was denotified for the purpose of resettling these people. Mandav is inhabited by the Koli Barias, which are politically more powerful and better-off than the Adivasis of Sagtala. The displaced Naik farmers built their homes in Sagtala, but cultivated the land in Mandav for some 4 years. In the fifth year, the people of Mandav village came with weapons and forbade the Sagtala displaced from farming there. The Naik farmers applied to the Collector, the forest department and the *Mamlatdar*, and also filed police complaints. Yet all official avenues of regaining physical possession of this land led nowhere. All the authorities shirk responsibility claiming that the land is the Naiks on paper, thus there is nothing further that they can do to enforce implementation. The Naiks now work as farm labour for Rs. 25 per day in their neighbours' fields, and migrate to cities to make ends meet. 'The government is slowly killing us by starvation', said Madhu Chuna. This highlights the manner in which apparent disputes between private parties are in fact due to state inaction. *Devgadh Mahila Sangathan* and Anandi have been fighting alongside this community to get justice.

4

Nature of Land Use

Land use among Adivasis in Gujarat has gone through pattern shifts from a primary reliance on foraging and swidden[19] agriculture, to later settled subsistence agriculture, and more recently a shift towards cash crop production. Despite these gradual transformations, Adivasis still rely on a land-based economy. In southern Gujarat, irrigation has prompted Adivasi cultivators to focus on sugarcane, bananas, and vegetables to be sold in local markets. Small farmers have stopped growing a diversity of paddy and other local millets and instead grow more conventional varieties of white paddy that may be sold easily in the markets. This represents a major change in the purely subsistence mentality of prior generations of cultivators. The loss of diversity is not captured by census data that homogenises 'paddy' and 'cereals' into single large categories. The dairy cooperative movement promoted by various voluntary institutions has driven a shift to fodder production for dairy cattle, resulting in neglect of cultivation of foodstuffs. These changes in land use represent an ad hoc adjustment to the mainstream economic framework and cultural ideals by shifting away from foraging and hunting to focus on agriculture.

Though Adivasis have been displaced from their traditional lands in many cases, agriculture is not displaced from the lives of Adivasi communities. According to census data on occupational status, even those Adivasis who occupy urban centres tend to rely on agriculture – either as labour or as a cultivator – to meet livelihood needs (see Figures 7 and 8).

19. Otherwise called slash and burn cultivation, podu, jhum etc.

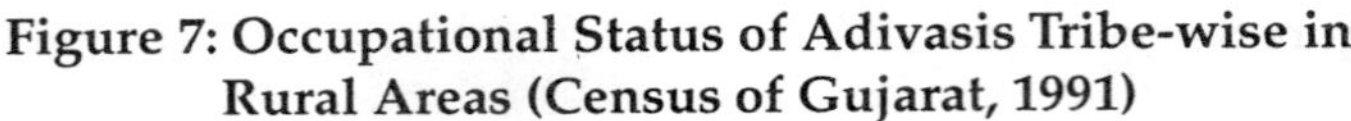

Figure 7: Occupational Status of Adivasis Tribe-wise in Rural Areas (Census of Gujarat, 1991)

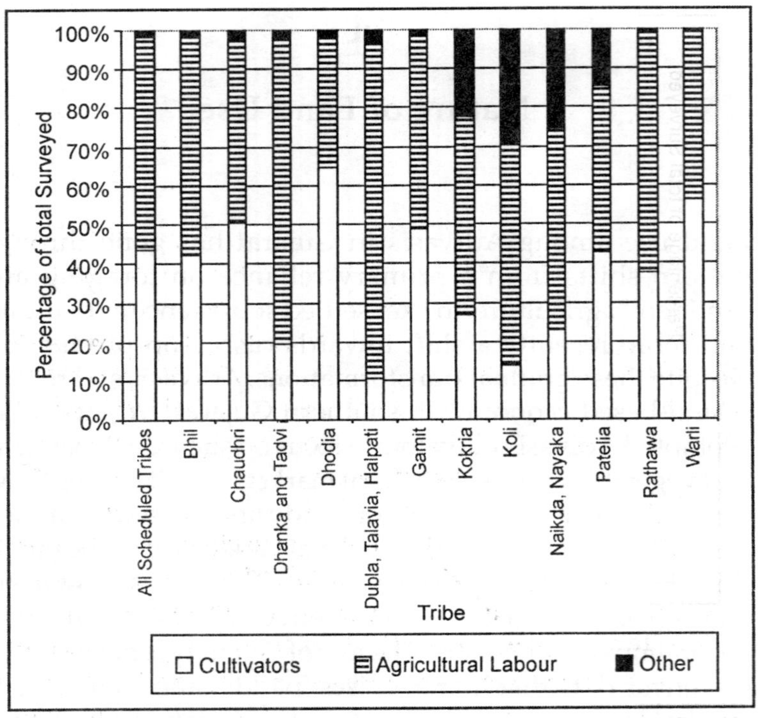

The Agricultural Census of India data suggests that a total of 9,52,971 ha are cultivated by the ST population in Gujarat, and is divided up into 861,554 holdings (see Table 23). This yields an average holding size of 1.06 ha amongst the Gujarat ST population. This is less than half of the average land holding size found in a sample survey done for the Government of Gujarat by Trivedi in 1980, who found the average land holding to be 2.43 ha.

Figure 8: Occupational status of Adivasis Tribe-wise in Urban Areas (Census of India, 1991)

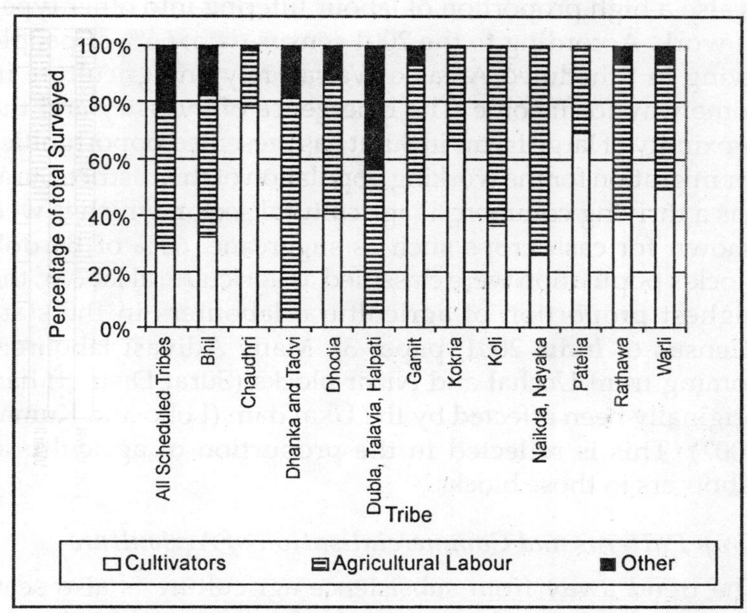

Table 23: 2001 Land Holdings and Area Amongst Scheduled Tribes in Gujarat

Size Class(HA)	*No. of Holdings*	*Irrigated Area*	*Unirrigated Area*	*Total Area*
Marginal (less than 1 ha)	1,79,126	10,117	61,193	71,310
Small (1-2 ha)	2,26,079	24,434	1,48,320	1,72,754
Semi-medium (2-4 ha)	2,52,279	37,640	2,54,152	2,91,792
Medium (4-10 ha)	1,78,914	38,058	2,92,137	3,30,195
Large (10 ha or larger)	25,156	8,290	78,630	86,920
ALL CLASSES	8,61,554	1,18,539	8,34,432	9,52,971

(Agricultural Census 2001)

The 2001 census reports that Bharuch (39.71%) and Narmada (45.59%) have the highest proportion of agricultural labourers to total workforce (see Table 22), which reflects that the economies of the region are still land-based. However, the proportion of self-cultivators is less than in other regions. Due to the number of industrial centres in the region, there is also a high proportion of labour filtering into other types of work. According to the 2001 census data, 66% of people living in Scheduled Areas of Valsad rely on agriculture in some way for income. The emergence of industry and the proximity of large farms in Surat has presented opportunities for migration for the working population of this district. Surat has a thriving commercial agricultural sector, which is well known for cash crops such as sugarcane. 63% of Bardoli block's population were classified as agricultural labour, the highest proportion of agricultural labourers in the state (Census of India 2001, paper 3). Many Adivasi labourers coming from Ucchal and Nizar blocks (Surat District) had originally been affected by the Ukai dam (Lobo and Kumar 2007). This is reflected in the proportion of agricultural labourers in those blocks.

Crop Patterns and Commercialisation of Agriculture

The trend away from subsistence agriculture is also seen through the decreasing area under food crop cultivation. In all of Gujarat, land under food crop cultivation has decreased by about 41.22 lakh hectares while area under non-food crop cultivation has increased by 87.65 lakh hectares. In scheduled areas, land under food crop cultivation has declined by nearly 8% in two decades, going from 548.71 lakh ha in 1980 to 507.5 lakh ha in 1999. This decline is partially due to the heavy environmental burden of chemical industries that render land unsuitable for cultivation. Where food crop cultivation continues, cereals, paddy and sugarcane account for the majority (92%) of cropped area in scheduled farmland (see Table 24). In fact, the 1991 Agricultural Census reports that Adivasi farmers contributed significantly to sugarcane and fodder production in the nation (see Table 25). Ironically, this covers both the high and low end of the economic spectrum. Gujarat ST cultivators also produced notable proportions of cotton and groundnut.

Table 24: Principle Crops among ST farmers

	Irrigated Area	*Unirrigated Area*	*Total Area*
Cereal	44064	557403	601467
Sugarcane	47123	0	47123
Paddy	16210	214061	230271

Agricultural Census 2001

Table 25: Gujarat's Contribution in Various Crop Production Amongst India's Scheduled Tribes

Crop	*Irrigated (%)*	*Unirrigated (%)*	*Total (%)*
Cotton	5.4	9.3	8.9
Sugarcane	37.1	8.3	32.0
Fodder	12.5	22.0	21.7
Groundnut	8.5	8.3	8.6
Jute	negligible	2.2	2.1
Lentils	1.6	1.6	1.6
Paddy	1.3	3.6	3.2

(Agricultural Census report for 1991)

Irrigation, both within and outside the Adivasi community, has transformed the entire logic of agriculture by changing the economic profitability of cash crops. On the one hand only a few cultivators have access to irrigation, and on the other, the traditional Adivasi resource base has plummeted, creating a situation that motivates and facilitates large farmers to exploit Adivasi labour. While Adivasis are the most highly displaced due to water works projects, they receive the fewest benefits. Only 12% of the total area cultivated by Adivasis is irrigated (see Figure 9). Of the total irrigated in area in Gujarat, the Adivasi share is merely 5%. About 81% of Adivasi holdings are totally unirrigated, 9% are completely irrigated, and 10% are partially irrigated. The likelihood of irrigation dramatically increases with land holding size (Agricultural Census, 1995-96). Commercial agriculture is practiced only among the small fraction of Adivasis who are able to irrigate their fields, primarily in the southern districts of Surat, Valsad, and Navsari.

Figure 9: Irrigation Pattern Among STs by Land Holding Size

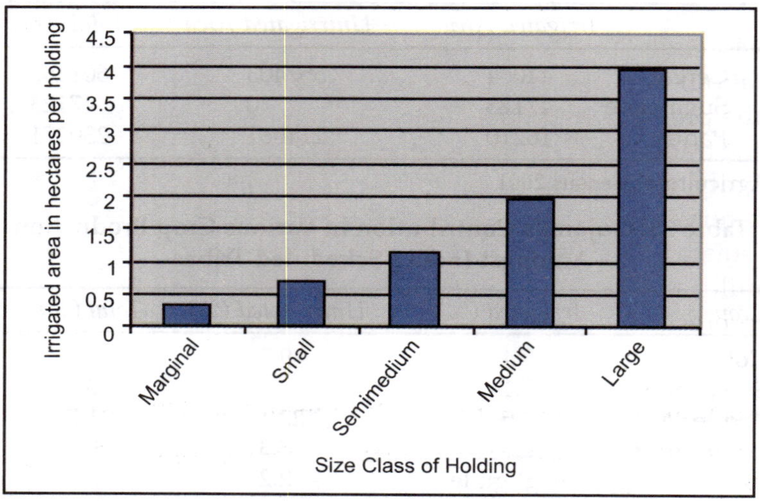

Data drawn from Agricultural census, 2001.

The surge in sugarcane plantation in south Gujarat is a prime example of how the economy of Adivasis is affected in multiple ways by the fact that access to irrigation and other resources is confined to a small minority. In 8 villages of Bardoli block, land under sugarcane production rose an average of 398% in the decade of 1965-75 (Breman 1994). The stable profit that sugarcane seems to provide to farmers and processors is behind this trend. Sugarcane cooperatives have been formed on a grand scale. Though in Surat district most of the leaders of the cooperatives are Kanbi Patidars, some Adivasi Chaudharies are also involved in the sugarcane commercialisation. The Kanbi Patidars, well organised and affluent, made up the leadership of the *Khedut Samaj* (a powerful farmers' lobby), and also hold positions on the boards of sugarcane factories. Since only large land holders have a chance at forming a cooperative or remaining on its board, the Adivasis who are primarily small-land holders are as a class excluded from the riches of this process. Sugarcane demands relatively little labour given its output.

The landless Adivasis – especially the Halpatis – have little chance of benefiting from the expansion of this crop. Moreover, in the early years of the sugarcane cooperatives labour was recruited exclusively from Maharashtra under the pretence that those workers were already familiar with the trade. In an effort to reduce the possibility for caste-class unity, as well as pre-empt the possibility of government intervention, the cooperatives have begun hiring some Gujarati Adivasis. Overall, these Adivasis are found to be mild and obedient and therefore non-threatening to the interests of the capitalist farmers (Breman 1994).

5

Conclusions

The Adivasi connection with land is intimate and remains the basis of their economy and culture. However their relationship with land has been disturbed by colonial conquest and later by the development paradigm set by the Indian state. In Gujarat, we see a familiar pattern of resource exploitation and wealth extraction that has set a worldwide trajectory for the indigenous experience in the contemporary era. Modern institutions of governance reinforce the power of the dominant classes while further marginalising the original settlers of these lands. The current condition of Adivasis in the state discredits the notion that 'overall' economic development can elevate the economic status of the lowest rung; the fact is that the lowest rung remains the lowest rung. Right now Adivasis are neither fully integrated into mainstream society, nor have they been left to 'develop according to their own genius' as some of the nation's leaders had envisioned.

The disparity in the condition of Adivasis and the upper-castes is highly pronounced in Gujarat. Whereas Gujarat boasts of being a highly industrialised state and a beacon of development in contemporary India, Adivasis have been left out of this economic 'growth'. Neither the emergence of the independent Indian state, nor the formation of present-day Gujarat has led to a legal framework in which the rights of Adivasis over their historical resources are recognised. They have been excluded from the democratic process and hardly considered worthy of self-determination. Again and again the historical literature refers to the 'animal like' or 'child like' nature of the Bhils, who have been patronised as if they are wards of the state rather than citizens. This attitude persists in the modern socio-political context and has had a lasting impact on Adivasi communities. The sociologist Shiv Visvanathan points out that for Adivasis in India, 'The drama of common access and common maintenance is now over. It is the ultimate paradox of anthropology where the native becomes outlaw in his own land. We face the paradox of a constitution that criminalises its own citizens' (Vishvanathan 2006).

Overall, the emerging picture is one of perpetual injustice. Gujarat state has a history of forfeiting the interest of the people for the sake of 'broader' state goals. The process of 'development'-induced resource dispossession is not unique to Gujarat nor to Adivasis, yet we see that Adivasis are disproportionately affected in Gujarat. Common and private land depletion and alienation are not simple economic issues but also a major socio-political problem. Adivasi culture and tradition has historically protected forest resources and promoted sustainable use of land. It is a great irony that these carefully used resources were then exploited by outsiders who simultaneously made the Adivasis victims of economic prosperity in Gujarat. The above is not the isolated story of just Adivasis, but of many communities in Gujarat who are victimised by the current development paradigm.

Glossary of Acronyms and Vernacular Terms

Ankabandhi system	A tax system in which traditional leaders collected taxes every few years from the entire village
Bigha	Unit of land area; 2327 sq. meters
BLRC	Bombay Land Revenue Code (BLRC)
Boodhan	Land gift movement led by Vinoba Bhave
CBO	Community based organisation
Chakars	Agricultural labourers in the fields of non-Adivasis
Darbar	Chieftan or local state
DFO	District Forest Officer
EIA	Environmental Impact Assessment
Eksali lease	Annual lease
Farati	Rotating
FCA	Forest Conservation Act 1980
FD	Forest Department
FSO	Forest Settlement Officer
Ghar Jamai	A man who resides with his wife's family
GIDC	Gujarat Industrial Development Corporation (GIDC)
GoG	Government of Gujarat
GOI	Government of India
GR	Government Resolution
Gunthas	Unit of land area; 121 sq yards
ha	Hectare
Khede teni jamin	Meaning Land to the Tiller in Gujarathi
IGF	Inspector General of Forests
IPT	Indian People's Tribunal
ITDP	Integrated Tribal Development Project
Jagirdari	System of land control by Jagirdars
Jagirdars	Grantees of Princely land

Juni sharat	Literally 'old condition', referring to legally unrestricted tenure
Khalsa	Unoccupied land assumed to be under state domain
Khatedars	Land owners
Kisan Sabha	Peasant organisation
Kisan	Farmer
Mamlatdar	Executive officer in charge of a block
MoEF	Ministry of Environment and Forest
Nagli	A millet type grain
Nallahs	Small stream
Narwadi-Bhagdari system	System in which village is taxed collectively
Navi sharat	Literally 'new condition', referring to legally restricted tenure
NGO	Non-governmental organisation
Panch	Council of five
Police patel	Village headman
Pucca	Concrete construction
Raasti	'Civilised' non-Adivasi
Raniparaj	Forest people
Ryotwari system	The system in which the cultivator directly held land and paid taxes to the state
Sarpanch	Elected head of the gram panchayat
Sarvodaya movement	Collective action toward achieving the ideals espoused by Gandhi
Satyagraha	Non-violent resistance to assert truth
ST	Scheduled Tribe
Talati	Village level secretary
Talukdari tenure	The occupant has non-inheritable rights to minerals, mines and trees
Tendu	A type of leaf used in bidis
UT	Union Territory
Vavli	Some immovable property, usually land, set aside specifically for a woman

References

1. ARCH vs. State of Gujarat and Others, 2005. Special Civil Application No. 9183/2005.
2. Avinash, 2005. *Background to the Forest Issue in Dangs District Gujarat.*
3. Awasthi, D, 2000. *Recent Changes in Gujarat Industry*, Economic and Political Weekly, Aug 26-Sept 2, 3183-3192.
4. Bose, Pradip Kumar, 1981. *Stratification among Tribals in Gujarat*, Economic and Political Weekly, 16(9): 191- 196.
5. Breman, Jan, 1994. *Wage Hunters and Gatherers*, Oxford University Press: New Delhi.
6. Breman, Jan, 1999. *Silencing the Voice of Agricultural Labourers in South Gujarat*, Modern Asian Studies, Vol. 33, No. 1, pp. 1-22.
7. Census of India, 2001. Gujarat State, paper 3.
8. Pinto, Stany. *Communalisation of Tribals in South Gujarat.*
9. Bijoy, C R, 2001. *Adivasi of India – A History of Discrimination, Conflict and Resistance*, Indigenous Affairs, International Work Group for Indigenous Affairs, 1/01, pp. 54-61.
10. Desai, K, 2002. *Land Reforms through People's Movements*, Land Reforms in India, Vol. VIII, Shah and Sah, eds., Sage Publications: New Delhi.
11. Desai, M B, 1958. *Report on Enquiry into the Working of the Bombay Tenancy and Agricultural Land Act, 1948 (as amended up to 1953) in Gujarat (Excluding Baroda District)*, The Indian Society of Agriculture Economics: Bombay.
12. Desai, M B, 1971. *Tenancy Abolition and the Emerging Pattern in Gujarat*, Department of Agriculture Economics, Baroda.
13. Dholakia, R, 2000. *Liberalisation in Gujarat: A Review of Recent Experience*, Economic and Political Weekly, Aug 26-Sept 2, pp. 3121-3124.
14. Dholakia, R, 2007. *Sources of Economic Growth and Acceleration*

in Gujarat, Economic and Political Weekly, Vol. XLII, No. 9, pp. 770-778.

15. Ekalavya Sangathan. *Does the Tribal Really Benefit? Tribal Sub-plan Analysis.*
16. Dogra, Bharat, nd. *Conquering Fear, Protecting Livelihood.* Social Change Papers, New Delhi.
17. Ekalavya – *Manav bina rahoni prashna puri pade che* (Ekalavya Sangathan, Disha).
18. Campaign for Survival and Dignity, 2003. *Endangered Symbiosis: Evictions and India's Forest Communities.*
19. Engineer, Irfan, 2002. *Struggles of Dangi Adivasis for Livelihood and Land*, Land Reforms in India, Vol. VIII, Shah and Sah, eds., Sage Publications: New Delhi.
20. Fernades, Walter (Forthcoming). *The Human Cost of Development-induced Displacement.*
21. Forest Survey of India, 2001.
22. Gujarat GR's relating to forest land; compiled by Disha, 1967-2005.
23. Hardiman, David, 2003. *Power in the Forest: The Dangs, 1820-1940*, Subaltern Studies VIII, Hardiman and Arnold, eds. Oxford University Press: New Delhi.
24. Pathy, Jaganath. *Impact of Development Projects on Adivasi Peoples.*
25. Indian People's Tribunal on Environment and Human Rights, 2004. *Narmada.*
26. IPT report on Gujarat pollution.
27. Iyengar. *Issues in Agricultural Development in a Tribal Area – A Study of Panchmahals District.*
28. Iyengar, Sudarshan, 2002. *Common Property Land Resources in Gujarat*, Land Reforms in India Vol. VIII, Shah and Sah, eds., Sage Publications: New Delhi, pp. 464-497.
29. Jani, Gaugrang and Varsha Ganguly, 2000. *Problem of Land Alienation Among Tribals of Gujarat*, Adivasi Gujarat, Vol. 10(2).
30. Jani, Indukumar, 2002. *Land Struggle in Eastern Gujarat*, Land Reforms in India Vol. VIII, Shah and Sah, eds., Sage Publications: New Delhi, pp. 349-376.
31. Joshi, Satyakam, 1997. *Development, Deprivation and Discontent: A Case of Dangs Tribals*, No. 21.
32. Judge, Paramjit, 1999. *Social Change through Land Reforms*, Rawat Publications: Jaipur and New Delhi.

33. *Jungle jamin khedta adivasio par junglekhatanu daman*, Adivasi Mahasabha's Fact finding report (in Gujarati).
34. Koshy, V C, *Land Reforms in India under the Plans*, Social Scientist, Vol. 2(12), 1974: 43-61.
35. Lal, R B, 1992. *From Farm to Factory*, Tribal Research and Training Institute, Gujarat Vidhyapeeth, Ahmedabad.
36. *Land Resources and Matrimonial Rights of Muslim Women*, Consult for Women and Land Rights, New Delhi.
37. Lobo, Lancy and Shashikant Kumar, 2007. *Development Induced Displacement in Gujarat (1947-2004), A summary report for the National Workshop*, Centre for Culture and Development.
38. Masavi, Mustaali, nd. *Problem of Land Alienation Among Tribals of Gujarat*, Tribal Research and Training Institute, Ahmedabad.
39. Mazgaonkar, M, 2004. *Letter to The Chairman of the Environment Public Hearing Committee*, Bharuch District, October 22, 2004, Subject: GMDC's Mining Plans relating to Amod Lease.
40. Ministry of Rural Development, 2006. *Report of the Expert Group on Prevention of Alienation of Tribal and its Restoration*, Government of India: New Delhi.
41. Modak, D S, 1932. Bombay Land System and Village Administration, Oriental Watchman Publishing House: Poona.
42. Mosse, David, et al. 2000. Brokered Livelihoods: Debt, Labour Migration and Development in Tribal Western India, *The Journal of Development Studies, Special Issue on Labour Mobility and Rural Society.* 38 (5): 59-88.
43. Pandya, Gaurish, and Arun Patel. *Indebtedness and Land Alienation Among the Tribals of Dadra Nagar Haveli.*
44. Parekh, Trupti, 2003. *Keepers of Forest: Foresters or Forest Dwellers?*
45. Parekh, Trupti, 2004. *Who is Destroying the Forests and Livelihood of Tribals? A Case of the Shoolpaneshwar Sanctuary*. Unpublished.
46. Patel, Girish, 2006. *Letter to the Principal Chief Conservator of Forest, Gujarat*, in relation to Sp Civil App filed by Adivasi Mahasabha.
47. Patel, Girishbhai. Personal interview dated 27 January 2007.
48. Pinto, Stany, nd. *Land Alienation and Consciousness Among the Vasavas of South Gujarat*, PhD Thesis, Centre for Social Studies, South Gujarat University.
49. Prasad, R R and M P Jahagirdar, 1993. *Tribal Situation in Forest Villages*, Discovery Publishing House: New Delhi.

50. *Report on Agricultural Census 1990-91*, Department of Agriculture and Cooperation, Ministry of Agriculture, Government of India.
51. Shah, A M, 2003. *The Tribes-So Called-of Gujarat: In the Perspective of Time*, Economic and Political Weekly, Vol. 38, No. 2, pp. 95-97.
52. Shah, G, 1986. *Stratification Among the Scheduled Tribes in the Bharuch and Panch Mahals Districts of Gujarat*, In: *Determinants of Social Status*, S C Malik, ed., Indian Institute of Advanced Studies: Shimla.
53. The Government of Gujarat, 1976. *Evaluation Study of Impact on Land Reform Measures in Gujarat State*, Directorate of Evaluation: Gandhinagar.
54. The Government of India, 1966. *Implementation of Land Reforms.*
55. The Planning Commission of India, 1966. *Implementation of Land Reforms: A Review by the Land Reforms Implementation Committee of the National Development Council.*
56. Stany Pinto. *Tribals in India: A People Betrayed, Dominated, Damned.*
57. Trivedi, H, 1993. *Tribal Land Systems: Land Reform Measures and Development of Tribals*, Concept Publishing Company: New Delhi.
58. Trivedi, Harshad, 1980. *Report of Land Systems of Tribal Areas of India with Special Reference to Tribal Areas of Gujarat*, Indian Institute of Public Administration: New Delhi.
59. Vasavda, Shilpa, 2006. *Enabling Women's Ownership over Private Land*, Paper presented at the Working Group for Women and Land Ownership State Level Seminar, Nov 16-17, Ahmedabad.
60. Vasavda, Shilpa. *Enabling Women's Ownership over Private Land*, WGWLO Workshop.
61. WGWLO 2004. *Study on Status of Women and Agriculture Land Ownership in Gujarat.*
62. Wood, John, 1984. *British versus Princely Legacies and the Political Integration of Gujarat*, Journal of Asian Studies, Vol. 44 (1): 64-99.
63. Xavier, Manjooran. *Forest Statistics Information*, Unpublished.